ON THE TRAIL

Sacramento Valley and Surrounding Mountains

JOHN ELLIOTT

PAGE PUBLISHING, INC.
Conneaut Lake, PA

First originally published by Page Publishing 2019

Photos on pages 16, 24, 51, 65, 92, 109, 132 and Back Cover are
courtesy of Steve Padalino.
All other photos are by John Elliott.
Front cover—Sierra Buttes
Back cover—Bald Rock

ISBN 978-1-68456-866-6 (pbk)
ISBN 978-1-68456-867-3 (digital)

Printed in the United States of America

For Julie Stark and Sharyl Simmons of Sutter County Museum, and everyone else who pushed me to publish this.

For those who accompanied me: Steve Padalino, Henry Greene, Peggy Wardle, Karrell Hickman, David Peña, Aragorn Aall, Jerry Nierengarten, Adrien Strasser, Hazel Hughes; my sisters and brother, Lisa, Victoria, and James; my parents, Maxine and Jack Elliott; and many more.

For Ryan Pope, so he can know where to take his buddies. And for my guardian angel, Arold Houtterseat.

INTRODUCTION

For many, the Sacramento Valley is that colorless adjunct to the San Joaquin Valley mirroring it to the south. The larger valley is a reflection by distortion. From a vehicle rushing through on the highway, both parts of California's Great Central Valley appear flat, featureless, monotonous, and bland. It is left to northern residents and those who take the time to discover that the Sacramento Valley can match any of the more famously scenic regions in a state notable for unique landscapes.

Surrounded by mountains on three sides, with the Sacramento–San Joaquin river delta to the south, the valley becomes Big Sky country when the regular winds clean out the haze. Crisp, white clouds scut across a royal-blue sky. Mountain crests etch the horizon in nearly every direction. I can stand in one spot on the valley floor, turning in a nearly complete circle, and see several peaks and summits where I have set foot.

In January, the hills are typically green, the waterfalls are full, and birds fill the wetlands. Wildflowers show up in February. In March orchards blossom across the valley. The wildflowers become serious in late March into April. In May the temperatures rise, the flowers fade, and the hills turn brown until next rainy season. The high country becomes accessible in stages—some trails still have snow in June and July. Wildflower season begins at the higher elevations. The best time for high-country lakes and summits is August and September. First snow is in October, and soon the high country is closed for the year. November brings autumn colors to the hills and valley. In December, rain is expected, and the last of the leaves come down. Millions of birds in the valley wetlands make this a bird-watcher's paradise. And it begins all over again.

Like much of California, there is somewhere to go year-round. The casual visitor will find the northern third of this hyperactive state to be quieter, less traveled, even uncrowded.

This guide is only that, an orientation to what lies available for exploration. It is by no means "complete." Every trail in this guide has been accomplished as a day trip from my home in the valley. No place here is too inaccessible for a pleasant, unrushed outing. My sincere apologies to those who feel I have betrayed their "secret spot." Many local trails are unmentioned, and new paths are being blazed every year. Even familiar paths can offer new discoveries and insights.

Don't be deceived by the big, flat valley seemingly filled with agriculture everywhere. There are scenic secrets and picturesque sites in every direction, some in plain view. All it takes is to head a few feet or more down any path that beckons, much as the rabbit hole appeared to Alice.

CONTENTS

HIKES

E = Easy stroll
M = Moderate, not too strenuous, but some effort required
S = Strenuous (C = steep climb, L = length)

Hike (High Point)   Miles   Rating   Features

Sacramento Valley—Though seemingly flat, the valley rises in elevation from near-sea level in the south near the delta to five hundred feet in the north at Redding. At first glance, the valley appears to offer only orchards, rice fields, and small farm towns bounded by levees. But being part of the Pacific Flyway, the opportunities to view wildlife make the Sacramento Valley a bird-watcher's paradise. (The Sutter Buttes, that anomaly of a small mountain range rising in the heart of the valley; actually, the eroded remains of a long-extinct volcano has no public access except in guided hikes led by local organizations. For that reason, it is not covered here.)

Sacramento Valley

Ellis Lake
Feather River Parkway

Hammon Grove Trail

Bobelaine Audubon Sanctuary

Gray Lodge Wildlife Area
Colusa National Wildlife Refuge
Colusa Riverfront
Sutter National Wildlife Refuge

Sacramento National Wildlife Refuge
Wetlands Trail
Logan Creek

Cosumnes River Preserve

Gray Lodge Wildlife Area

Ellis Lake (52')   1   E   *Urban lake, waterfowl, reclaimed marsh*

Designed by Golden Gate Park master gardener, John McLaren, this is the crown jewel of Marysville. After a stroll on the paved path around the lake, it is pleasant to wander down D Street, through Marysville's historic gold rush downtown to the unique Bok Kai Temple tucked in at the levee. From the top of the levee, the Yuba River flows below in its final approach to the Feather River.

Directions: Located in the heart of Marysville, with D Street on the west, Fourteenth Street on the north, B Street on the east, and Ninth Street on the south, the best access is from D Street at Twelfth Street.

Feather River Parkway (52')   0.5–5   E   *Riparian woods, birds, wildlife, handicapped access to river view*

This former river bottomland is now threaded with winding trails, including a paved path which allows handicapped access to a view of the Feather River. Besides the woodlands, there are reedy grasslands and a pond. The trail from the picnic tables at the south end of the parking lot leads most directly to the easily accessed sandy river beaches. Dogs are permitted on leash.

Directions: Heading east on Highway 20 (Colusa Avenue) Yuba City, take the Sutter Street exit and turn left on Sutter Street, passing under Highway 20. Just past the Stop sign, turn right on Lamon Way, then right on Von Geldern Way, continuing over the levee into the park. Coming from Marysville on Highway 20, take the first exit off the bridge and right onto Market Street, turning right again very shortly onto Lamon Way.

Hammon Grove Trail (250') 1 E *Dry Creek, valley woodland, Yuba River access*

There aren't extensive trails here, but Hammon Grove Park, together with Sycamore Ranch next door, is the site of a former Maidu village. If you wander from Dry Creek to the broad Yuba River, it makes sense, with a cooling canopy of oak woodland and abundant salmon from the river, that a settlement here is a no-brainer. A nice one-mile loop signed for the trail begins near the barbecue area. For a short distance, the wide path rambles beside Dry Creek, large sycamores providing a scenic frame on both sides of the creek. Autumn is especially nice when the vivid gold foliage is reflected in the creek's placid surface. I would dare to suggest that in those brief glorious days of autumn, this quarter mile is the prettiest spot in the county—and Yuba County is a beautiful place.

After the path swings away from Dry Creek, it gradually rises through a blue oak woodland. Along this section of trail, a gravel path cuts through the shady woodland to a floating walkway across Dry Creek to Sycamore Grove—formerly a private campground, now a county park. Continuing on the loop, the trail crosses a parking area and descends to Yuba River access, the halfway point on the loop. Across the broad, swiftly flowing river, the dark mounds of the Yuba Goldfields sit like a desolate no-man's-land. From the river access, the trace of an old road wanders about a quarter mile along the river bluff to the mouth of Dry Creek. The return portion of the loop traverses the eastern edge of the park. An alternate route here is the disc golf course, with its pole-and-chain-baskets set along a winding route, but only if no one is playing.

Directions: Located on Highway 20, about twelve miles east of Marysville, on the right one mile past the Marysville Road turnoff.

Bobelaine Sanctuary (45') 0.05–5 E *Lakes, riparian woods, savannahs, old-growth trees, wildlife, view where Bear River enters Feather River*

This is a true treasure of the valley—a hint as to how it looked before settlers turned most of the valley into farmland. Five miles of easy trails wander by lakes, and through old-growth woodlands and broad, grassy savannahs. Though this is next to the Feather River, the river is mostly not visible, and the only spot with a clear view of the river is a high bank viewpoint looking across to where the Bear River enters the Feather. Named for Bob and Elaine Crandall, the largest lake here is called Crandall Lake. As this is an Audubon preserve, dogs are not permitted, but bird-watching is a plus.

Directions: Located approximately twelve miles south of Yuba City, near Dingville, turn from Highway 99 onto Laurel Avenue, and head toward the levee. Continue at the end of Laurel on what is a private road but allows access to the parking area at the foot of the levee.

Gray Lodge Wildlife Area (62') 2.5 E *Wetlands, birds, wildlife, view of Sutter Buttes and surrounding mountain ranges*

The two-mile hiking path, on maintenance roads, is completely flat. The half-mile route to a raised observation deck is paved and wheelchair-accessible. One gets a sense of what the valley was like before it was tamed by settlers. From November through January, this is the Yosemite of bird-watching. Day-use fees.

Directions: Take Pennington Road from Highway 99 in Live Oak east toward Sutter Buttes. Follow signs to Gray Lodge. Turn left (west) at main entrance and follow paved road two miles to visitor parking. (Fee: four dollars per person)

Colusa NWR (59') 1 E *Wetlands, wildlife, birds*

The trail begins just across the small auto bridge signed for Wetlands Discovery Trail. The path is mostly a grass corridor through stands of willow and cottonwood, with wetlands stretching away to the west. At about 0.3 mile, a side path cuts to the left to a visible observation deck, which provides a bench for enjoying the view of the wetlands, with Snow Mountain and the Coast Range looming to the west. Shortly beyond this, the main trail bends and continues under power lines. A half mile from the trailhead, the path ends at a footbridge, which might have been an observation deck once, but is now a footbridge to nowhere, with the wetlands barely visible through the brush. Highway 20, which borders the refuge on the north, is never out of sight or sound, but doesn't detract much from the peace of the wetlands.

Directions: Located on Highway 20, just west of Colusa, on the south side of the highway. Use the parking area for hikers.

Colusa Riverfront (59')   1–2   E   *Sacramento River, riparian woodland, historic Colusa*

Walk along the levee, with the Sacramento River on one side and historic Colusa below on your left. Where the river bends to the north, you enter the grassy, shaded lawn of the state recreation area. Just past the boat-ramp parking area, an old road, now a path, winds through a peaceful wooded area for a half mile to a view of the river.

Directions: Take Highway 20 to Colusa. The levee is easily accessed from the bridge to the boat ramp.

Sutter NWR (50')   0.5–4   E   *Wetlands, wildlife, birds*

The trail begins at the parking kiosk. Cross the levee and then the concrete bridge. Follow the signs to the pond area. Access for wildlife is permitted February 15–June 30. By late spring, the wetlands have dried into a grassy prairie, and migrating fowl have moved on. The paths are well-mowed, wide, flat, and clearly marked. Besides the riparian areas along the side creeks, large Valley oaks dot the landscape. Stroll at will on any combination of a network of paths.

Directions: From Highway 99 south of Yuba City, take Bogue or Oswald roads to Schlag Road. Take Schlag Road to Hughes Road, and Hughes Road to the Sutter Bypass levee. Turn left onto the unpaved levee and follow the levee almost three miles to the parking kiosk to the left of the levee. It is permitted to drive across the concrete bridge to designated handicapped parking.

Sacramento NWR
Wetlands Trail (141')　2　E　*Wetlands, birds, wildlife*

This pleasant loop is flat and, except for the side trail along Logan Creek, wheelchair-accessible. Nearby I-5 is never out of earshot, but that doesn't detract from the beauty of the wetlands with its ever-present multitude of birds. The trail, signed as Wetlands Walk, begins on the path between the parking area and the visitor center. Maps and brochures are available at the trailhead. Across the maintenance road, the path branches to the right and then north by Logan Creek. Across the auto tour road, a scenic side trail follows the creek through riparian habitat, crossing simple footbridges, before rejoining the main trail. The rest of the loop provides expansive views of the wetlands and the surrounding mountains: Snow Mountain to the west, Lassen Peak to the northeast, and the Sutter Buttes as jagged relief on the flat horizon to the southeast. The peak season for bird-watching is November to January, but birds are found year-round. Dogs are allowed on leash. Day-use fees.

Directions: From I-5 south of Willows, take the Princeton / Road 68 exit, then north on the frontage road, Old Highway 99, to the wildlife refuge entrance.

Logan Creek (141')　3　E　*Wetlands*

From February 15 to June 30, mowed observation trails accessible from Road 68 are open along Logan Creek. Flat grassy paths meander along the narrow, winding creek and through vast wetlands that stretch to the horizon. In spring, wildflowers carpet the grasslands. Deer and year-round birds can be seen more easily than at the more popular main visitors' section, visible a few miles to the northwest. That would be perhaps the greatest feature of this walk—the solitude and the quiet sense of the valley as "Big Sky" country. The vista includes Snow Mountain due west, Lassen Peak's white cone to the northeast in the southern edge of the Cascades, and southeast the Sutter Buttes defy the valley's flat contours. For a three-mile loop (longer loops are possible in the trail system here), from the west corner of the parking area, take the path that briefly parallels the road and take the left choice at every trail junction.

Directions: From I-5 south of Willows, take the Princeton / Road 68 exit, Cross the frontage road and head east on Road 68 toward Princeton. The parking area is on the right 2.5 miles from I-5.

Cosumnes River Preserve (40')   0.25–4   E   *Wildlife, wetlands, river*

This isn't technically in the Sacramento Valley. It sits just east of the Delta, at the point where the Sacramento, and San Joaquin valleys meet. To see wildlife, you don't have to wander more than a few steps from your vehicle. But this is an opportunity to fully enjoy the tranquility of a rare, ancestral riparian area that has survived development on all sides.

The Delta has shifted from being an integral part of one the world's largest wetlands to being a leveed system of islands devoted to farming. For the full loop tour (on foot only, as there is no auto tour here), cross the footbridge adjacent to the visitor center and turn right at the trail junction. The rule of thumb for this hike is to take the right option at every junction. The loop takes you on route along the Cosumnes River through a heavily wooded riverside forest, representative of the dense habitat that historically grew along the area's waterways. The second half of the loop visits the wetlands and marshes that make up most of the preserve. In winter, the presence of the ostrichlike sand hill cranes makes this preserve unique among the valley's many wildlife refuges.

Directions: From I-5 south of Elk Grove, take the Twin Cities Road exit, also signed for Walnut Grove and Locke. Turn left and take Twin Cities Road to Franklin Road, also the first Stop sign. Turn right and travel one mile to the preserve visitor center.

Lower Foothills—Many look at the foothills as what you have to go through to get to the good stuff higher up. The trails may lack the overall grandeur of the High Sierra, but they are accessible year-round; even on the hottest summer days, early mornings are still pleasant. The vegetation at the lower elevations is predominately blue oak woodland, with stands of interior live oak, foothill pine, buckeye, and cottonwood. Huge valley oaks dot the grassy savannahs. This is the zone where you will find more predators (coyote, bobcat, mountain lion, hawks, and rattlesnakes) and poison oak thrives. As the elevation rises, the trees become a mix of pine, fir, and big leaf maples.

Hidden Falls Regional Park
Hidden Falls Loop
Sky Ridge Loop
South Legacy Way

Spenceville Wildlife Area
Fairy Falls
Little Dry Creek
Poppy Hill
Pittman Ridge Loop
Wood Duck Loop
Lookout Loop
Upper Jones Pond
Ditch Trail
Waldo Bridge
Four Ponds Loop (Horseshoe Pond)
Walsh Trail
Council Rocks
Rose Hill
Rock City

Black Swan Preserve
Black Swan Trail
Deer Creek Narrows

JOHN ELLIOTT

Daugherty Hill
Donovan Hill
Honcut Creek

North Table Mountain

Paradise Ridge
Bille Park
Upper Ridge Preserve
Magalia Greenbelt
Clotilde Merlo Park

Bidwell Park
Lower Bidwell Park
Monkeyface Rock
North Rim Loop
South Rim Trails

Upper Bidwell Park

Hidden Falls Regional Park—Seeming much larger than its 1,200 acres, this popular park offers waterfalls, dense woodland, and ridgetop vistas. Ranging across the narrow foothill canyons of Coon and Deadman Creeks, there are several options for hikes on the twenty-three-mile web-like network of trails. Venturing beyond Canyon View Bridge into the more remote, western section of the park on exceptionally well-designed trails makes for very long day hikes, which is why horse riders outnumber hikers in this area.

Due to its proximity to Delta breeze moisture, vegetation here is lusher and includes ponderosa pines on the shady slopes of Deadman Canyon. Rugged Coon Creek Canyon, and verdant Deadman Canyon have formed along the Foothill Fault that runs northeasterly through Camp Far West and Spenceville Wildlife Area to Oroville. Dogs are permitted on leash, which is a good idea, because there are a lot of dogs here. This is a very popular park on any given day, and on every trail, the walker may encounter other folks on horseback, bicycle, as well as foot.

Hidden Falls Loop (1,100')   5.1   M   *Waterfalls, foothill woodland, Coon Creek gorge, views*

It is simple to go directly to the falls, a round-trip of three miles, which is why there's usually lots of company on the trail. More satisfying is to patch bits of different trails together for a scenic circuit around the eastern older section of the park, including the falls. To reach any of this, you must descend into Deadman Canyon, on either the single-track Poppy Trail or the service road (South Legacy Way) one mile to the Whiskey Diggins Bridge across Deadman Creek.

A good loop option is to descend on the pretty Poppy Trail, which drops in a few switchbacks and follows the shady creek to the bridge, and later return on the broad road, which climbs more gradually and avoids the hordes barreling down the Poppy Trail. Cross the bridge, and shortly up the road is the turnoff on the left to the falls. Instead, take the turnoff to the right, Blue Oak Loop, a quiet path that winds through an oak woodland to the top of a small ridge, where you cross Turkey Ridge Road; and on the Seven Pools Vista Trail, drop on a gradual descent through oak woodland to the edge of Coon Creek Gorge and the Seven Pools Vista. From a rocky precipice, there is a great view of the gorge and the pools far below, connected by cascades and small waterfalls. Continue on the trail as it winds back along the wooded slope.

At the junction with the Seven Ponds Trail, turn right and drop to a creek-side trail that contours above the creek, mostly unseen. At the junction with the Turtle Pond Trail, turn right for creek access. Continue on the Seven Ponds Trail as it rises and winds away from the creek. Take the first right, Quail Run Trail, which winds to the top of the ridge, and a right on Blue Oak Loop soon brings you to the service road (North Legacy Way). Turn right, pass through the gate, and follow the road down to Canyon View Bridge high over Coon Creek. Look for the trail on the left side of the bridge signed for Hidden Falls.

It is worthwhile to visit the observation deck visible across the bridge for a fine view of Canyon View Falls. Continue on the Hidden Falls Access Trail a short distance to the trail on the right, which leads to the overlook for the park's scenic namesake waterfall, where Deadman Creek ruggedly drops to join Coon Creek. The thirty-foot falls run year-round, but are most impressive in spring. From here, it's an easy half mile along the access trail to the bridge over Deadman Creek and the climb back to the trailhead.

Directions: From Old Highway 65 between Lincoln and Sheridan, take W. Wise Road east toward the hills for 8.3 miles to the junction with Mt. Vernon Road. Where Wise Road turns right, continue straight on Mt Vernon Road, climbing into the hills for 2.8 miles to Mears Drive on the left. Turn onto Mears Drive and follow the signs a short distance to Hidden Falls Park.

Sky Ridge Loop (1,081')   0.7   M   *Views*

This short loop leaves the parking area on the west side of the restrooms. Though the parking area is never out of sight below, the views compensate for the lack of a "wilderness" experience. The trail winds to the grassy crest of the ridge, where on a clear day there is a panoramic vista of the entire south Sacramento Valley with the Coast

Range beyond and the Sutter Buttes to the north. Likewise, the view across the nearby Placer County foothills is pleasantly expansive. Descending from the ridge, there is the option of connecting to the handicapped-accessible Hidden Gateway Trail to return to the trailhead.

Directions: From Old Highway 65 between Lincoln and Sheridan, take W. Wise Road east toward the hills for 8.3 miles to the junction with Mt. Vernon Road. Where Wise Road turns right, continue straight on Mt. Vernon Road, climbing into the hills for 2.8 miles to Mears Drive on the left. Turn onto Mears Drive and follow the signs a short distance to Hidden Falls Park.

South Legacy Way (1,100')   4.5   M   *Foothill woodland, distant falls view*

This is the one trail within range of the parking area where it is less likely to encounter even a fraction of the hordes that throng here. It is also the shadiest trail. Take any route to Whiskey Diggins Bridge at Deadman Creek, but don't cross the bridge. Strike out on the ditch-tender's path signed for South Legacy Way. After a short distance on the flat graveled path, a single-track trail cuts to the right, through a gate and drops away from the ditch. This is part of the newer trail system constructed for the western sector of the park; well designed, the trail contours with the slope in an up-and-down pattern that highlights the trees and rocks.

All the while, Deadman Creek burbles merrily close below, though unseen through the low brush. Across the creek, the popular trail to Hidden Falls stands out like a busy gash along the hillside. At about a half mile, the falls and its observation deck can be glimpsed through the trees. Very soon, Coon Creek, its new bridge, and observation deck come into view.

Beyond this, it is another half mile to the junction with Pheasant Trail and the network of trails in the western sector. Along that half mile, across Coon Creek, much of the Creekside Trail is visible below, as well as the North Legacy Way road above. A circuit is possible by continuing on the South Legacy Trail to the footbridge and then returning on one of the north side trails, a route of seven-plus miles. There is a small grassy flat about one hundred yards before the Pheasant Trail junction, which makes a fine resting spot before retracing your steps.

Directions: From Old Highway 65 between Lincoln and Sheridan, take W. Wise Road east toward the hills for 8.3 miles to the junction with Mt. Vernon Road. Where Wise Road turns right, continue straight on Mt. Vernon Road, climbing into the hills for 2.8 miles to Mears Drive on the left. Turn onto Mears Drive and follow the signs a short distance to Hidden Falls Park.

Spenceville Wildlife Area—Most people go to Spenceville for Fairy Falls, never realizing there are miles of trails throughout the wildlife area's 11,942 acres. Numerous ponds attract all manner of wildlife. The Foothill Fault runs the length of the wildlife area, and most of the great rock outcroppings are found along it, at Jones and Pittman ridges, Rock City, Rose Hill, and especially Council Rocks.

Fairy Falls (600')   4   M   Waterfalls, blue oak woodland, Dry Creek gorge, grinding holes

Cross the bridge, turn right, follow old road and signs to Fairy Falls. Sixty-five-foot Upper Falls has a fenced-in vista point. Ten-foot Lower Falls is located midpoint in the falls gorge. Return on the unmarked creek trail for a loop. Ancient grinding holes can be found on large rock outcroppings, one in the meadow near the lower end of the creek trail and the other near the trailhead, down the creek across from the rope swing.

Directions: Take Hammonton Smartsville Road, fifteen miles from the Simpson Lane–traffic light, east to Chuck Yeager Road, and turn right. Or from Highway 20 in Smartsville, take Hammonton Smartsville Road, one mile to Chuck Yeager Road, and turn left. Take Chuck Yeager Road, 4.7 miles to unpaved Waldo Road, and turn left. Travel on unpaved Waldo Road to one-lane metal Waldo Bridge over Dry Creek. Beyond the bridge, turn left on Spenceville

Road and follow it 2.4 miles to trailhead parking by the concrete bridge. No restrooms at trailhead.

Little Dry Creek (400')   4   M   *Blue oak woodland*

From the trailhead, follow the route to Fairy Falls just a short distance to a latched single-person gate on the left just past the bridges over Little Dry Creek and the fenced-off, former toxic-waste site, which was home to the Spenceville copper mine. Follow the path beyond the gate as far as inclination allows, through a small valley shaded by large oaks. The route can be extended by taking paths east to Hatchet Creek Trail for a five-mile loop, or west over a wooded ridge to Pittman Wash for a four-mile loop.

Directions: Take Hammonton Smartsville Road, fifteen miles from the Simpson Lane–traffic light, east to Chuck Yeager Road, and turn right. Or from Highway 20 in Smartsville, take Hammonton Smartsville Road, one mile to Chuck Yeager Road, and turn left Take Chuck Yeager Road, 4.7 miles to unpaved Waldo Road, and turn left. Travel on unpaved Waldo Road to one-lane metal Waldo Bridge over Dry Creek. Beyond the bridge, turn left on Spenceville Road and follow it 2.4 miles to the Fairy Falls trailhead parking by the concrete bridge. No restrooms at trailhead.

Poppy Hill (1260')   4   M   *Highest point in Spenceville, views, golden poppy displays (spring)*

Not only is this the highest point at Spenceville, but the most breathtaking displays of golden poppies in the area are found covering the steep west slopes in springtime. Follow the trail to Fairy Falls, but where the trail turns left through a latched gate, stay straight ahead on the old ranch road beyond the locked gate. It is impossible to miss the poppy-covered hill rising ahead. Where the old road rises to wind behind the hill, look for a faint-use path, which follows the crest of the hill to its summit. Take this path and enjoy the panoramic views of Spenceville and vast expanses of wildflowers. Return the way you came, or connect with one of the other return routes from Fairy Falls.

Directions: Take Hammonton Smartsville Road, fifteen miles from the Simpson Lane–traffic light, east to Chuck Yeager Road, and turn right. Or from Highway 20 in Smartsville, take Hammonton Smartsville Road, one mile to Chuck Yeager Road, and turn left. Take Chuck Yeager Road, 4.7 miles to unpaved Waldo Road, and turn left. Travel on unpaved Waldo Road to one-lane metal Waldo Bridge over Dry Creek. Beyond the bridge, turn left on Spenceville Road and follow it 2.4 miles to the Fairy Falls trailhead parking by the concrete bridge. No restrooms at trailhead.

Pittman Ridge Loop (665') 5 M *Pittman Pond, meadows, blue oak woodland, Dry Creek narrows*

From the parking area, cross the concrete bridge and turn left, away from the Fairy Falls route. Take gravel Pittman Road a short distance to the creek-side picnic area with rope swing, and at the gate beyond, look for the unsigned path on the left side of the gate, which heads downstream along Dry Creek. After walking alongside Dry Creek riparian foliage for a short distance, you reach broad Pittman Wash and a trail that cuts to the right. Take this trail, or you can continue downstream and turn up the next draw, which leads you past three small ponds. The latter trail connects with the former, so either option ends up at Pittman Pond, largest pond at Spenceville.

On the west (left) side of the pond, the route continues up Pittman Wash to the ranch road at the top of the draw. Look for the well-used path, which cuts to the left in a more direct route to the gap. Wherever you reach the old road, turn left and take the road to the crest of the ridge. There is a circle of rocks north of the gap for a breather. Look for the path heading south on the ridge and continue on it along the wooded ridge crest. Views present themselves at points on what is a really pleasant stroll along the ridge. Following the crest as it drops rockily to Dry Creek lands you in the picturesque narrows, and from here you take the creek-side path upstream to the trailhead.

Directions: Take Hammonton Smartsville Road, fifteen miles from the Simpson Lane–traffic light, east to Chuck Yeager Road, and turn right. Or from Highway 20 in Smartsville, take Hammonton Smartsville Road, one mile to Chuck Yeager Road, and turn left. Take Chuck Yeager Road, 4.7 miles to unpaved Waldo Road, and turn left. Travel on unpaved Waldo Road to one-lane metal Waldo Bridge over Dry Creek. Beyond the bridge, turn left on Spenceville Road and follow it 2.4 miles to the Fairy Falls trailhead parking by the concrete bridge. No restrooms at trailhead.

Wood Duck Loop (629')   2.25   M   *Ponds, blue oak woodland*

From the single-person gate, take the single-track path away from the road to the small grove of trees visible up the drainage of Wood Duck Creek gurgling to your right. Lower Wood Duck Pond sits just beyond those trees. At the pond, follow the second, lower, single-track path on a very pleasant stroll up the rolling oak-forested canyon of Wood Duck Creek to Upper Wood Duck Pond. Though not as scenic as many of the Spenceville ponds, it does offer a great sitting spot on a log shaded by a huge valley oak. After enjoying the stillness, take the old wagon road in its gentle climb up and over the ridge, returning to the lower pond and trailhead, or on the road to the gate at the end of Spenceville Road.

Directions: Take Hammonton Smartsville Road, fifteen miles from the Simpson Lane–traffic light, east to Chuck Yeager Road, and turn right. Or from Highway 20 in Smartsville, take Hammonton Smartsville Road, one mile to Chuck Yeager Road, and turn left. Take Chuck Yeager Road, 4.7 miles to unpaved Waldo Road, and turn left. Travel on unpaved Waldo Road to one-lane metal Waldo Bridge over Dry Creek. Beyond the bridge, turn left on Spenceville Road and follow it 2.0 miles to a latched, single-person wooden gate on the right across the road from the closed metal gate of the camping area. Park on the side of the road. For another access, drive to the end of Spenceville Road, 0.1 miles past the Fairy Falls trailhead, and walk up the wagon road beyond the closed gate to the loop.

Lookout Loop (820')   3   M   *Pond, live oak woodland, views*

Though you climb to the top of a ridge, it's a relatively easy ascent. From the gate, walk up gravel Nichols Road through shady, live-oak groves, green even in winter. Where a locked gate signifies the wildlife area boundary, take the old wagon road to your right, past a few acres of plowed fields and little Spring Pilot Pond, to a locked metal gate near the ridgeline. Beyond the gate, turn right on the ridge trail, passing through a barbed-wire gate, and amble along the ridge with expanding views. A brief climb brings you to the flat-topped lookout, the site of a former watchtower.

Here a panoramic vista includes much of Spenceville and the Foothill Fault, angling south to north below you toward Browns Valley, Sacramento Valley, Sutter Buttes, and Coast Range. It's an easy one-mile descent on the old road to the junction with Nichols Road at the trailhead.

Directions: Take Hammonton Smartsville Road, fifteen miles from the Simpson Lane–traffic light, east to Chuck Yeager Road, and turn right. Or from Highway 20 in Smartsville, take Hammonton Smartsville Road, one mile to Chuck Yeager Road, and turn left Take Chuck Yeager Road, 4.7 miles to unpaved Waldo Road, and turn left. Travel on unpaved Waldo Road to one-lane metal Waldo Bridge over Dry Creek. Beyond the bridge, turn left on Spenceville Road and follow it 1.9 miles to a locked white metal gate on the right, just before reaching Wood Duck Creek and the camping area. Park on the side of the road; do not block the gate.

Upper Jones Pond (500')   0.5–4   E/M   *Pond, blue oak woodland, Foothill Fault*

It's an easy quarter mile from the trailhead to the pretty pond. A shaded, grassy hillside beside the pond makes a nice picnic site. Beyond the pond, turn right on the old wagon road to reach the ridgeline for access to both the second highest point at Spenceville and the lookout. There is access here too, to the flat gravel Jones Road, which runs in a straight line down the valley along the Foothill Fault. This is also the eastern terminus of the Ditch Trail (see next entry).

Directions: Take Hammonton Smartsville Road, fifteen miles from the Simpson Lane–traffic light, east to Chuck Yeager Road, and turn right. Or from Highway 20 in Smartsville, take Hammonton Smartsville Road, one mile to Chuck Yeager Road, and turn left Take Chuck Yeager Road, 4.7 miles to unpaved Waldo Road, and turn left. Travel on unpaved Waldo Road to one-lane metal Waldo Bridge over Dry Creek. Beyond the bridge, turn left on Spenceville Road and follow it 0.3 miles to Camp Far West Road. Turn right and follow Camp Far West Road, 1.7 miles to Long Ravine Road. Turn left on Long Ravine, 1.7 miles to a large pullout on the left with single-person chain-link gate, located 0.1 miles past the white metal gate at the southern terminus of Jones Road.

Ditch Trail (500')   0.5–5   E   *Ponds, blue oak woodland*

This is the easiest walk at Spenceville with the most scenic value. A flat trail follows the ditch, which channels water from Upper Jones Pond to the large unnamed pond near the trailhead. From the gate, follow the wagon road to the pond about one hundred yards away, but obscured by reeds. The path heading off uphill to the right at the trailhead is the return path from the Jones Road gate if a loop is desired. Circle around the pond to a locked metal gate at the northeast corner. Beyond the gate, follow the trail along the fence to the ditch trail and amble to your own satisfaction as you contour the shallow hills on a flat, wide path. Along the way are small ponds and views of the lookout up on Jones Ridge. If you reach Jones Road, there's the option of returning on the path, which parallels Long Ravine Road back to the trailhead.

Directions: Take Hammonton Smartsville Road, fifteen miles from the Simpson Lane–traffic light, east to Chuck Yeager Road, and turn right. Or from Highway 20 in Smartsville, take Hammonton Smartsville Road, one mile to Chuck Yeager Road, and turn left Take Chuck Yeager Road, 4.7 miles to unpaved Waldo Road, and turn left. Travel on unpaved Waldo Road to one-lane metal Waldo Bridge over Dry Creek. Beyond the bridge, turn left on Spenceville Road, and follow it 0.3 miles to Camp Far West Road. Turn right and follow Camp Far West Road, 1.7 miles to Long Ravine Road. Turn left on Long Ravine, 0.2 miles to a locked chain-link gate on the left. Park off the road by the gate; do not block it.

Waldo Bridge (253')   1.5   E   *Historic site, Dry Creek, blue oak woodland*

Beyond the green metal gate, follow the old Spenceville Road 0.5 mile before approaching the east boundary and residential housing of Beale AFB. You can also stroll along Dry Creek on a pleasant creek-side path. The area around the south end of the Waldo Bridge is the site of the former community of Waldo, which was initially settled by two black men who started selling vegetables from their garden to travelers on Spenceville Road.

Directions: Take Hammonton Smartsville Road, fifteen miles from the Simpson Lane–traffic light, east to Chuck Yeager Road, and turn right. Or from Highway 20 in Smartsville, take Hammonton Smartsville Road, one mile to Chuck Yeager Road, and turn left Take Chuck Yeager Road, 4.7 miles to unpaved Waldo Road, and turn left. Travel on unpaved Waldo Road to one-lane metal Waldo Bridge over Dry Creek. Park on the south side of the bridge; do not block the gate.

Four Ponds Loop (706')   3   M   *Ponds, blue oak woodland, Horseshoe Pond*

From the gate, walk up Pittman Road, a gravel maintenance road 0.5 mile to a junction of trails. The old wagon road heading up to the left is the southern terminus of the Walsh Trail; bypass it. A few yards farther, an old wagon road cuts to the right down the draw. This is one end of the Four Ponds Trail and will be your return route. For a loop, continue on the gravel road and return on the much more pleasant trail. (Or take the trail in and out, which is not a bad option.)

On Pittman Road, there is a nice view of the valley and Sutter Buttes as the road crests the ridge. Dropping steeply down the other side of the ridge, the road offers a nice glimpse of Poppy Hill and the eastern part of Spenceville. After crossing Cox Creek on a metal grate, take any of the next three paths to the left a short distance to Horseshoe Pond, second largest pond at Spenceville. Three picnic tables are placed here in a shady oak grove with a nice view of the pond. This is the sole location in all of Spenceville, where anything other than rocks or logs is provided for seating.

As such, it is one of the nicest destinations at Spenceville, to sit and enjoy the peace. To return via the trail, go to Cox Creek (the metal grate), cross the creek, and look for the single-track trail cutting off to the left. It briefly rises and falls before seriously, but not strenuously, climbing the southern flanks of the ridge you crossed earlier. After veering right (north) up the broad unnamed wash, it becomes the old wagon road noted earlier and passes the four ponds, which gave the trail its name. At the gravel road, turn left and return to your vehicle. The only drawback to the Four Ponds Trail portion of the loop is that the shooting range is never out of earshot, though no one is ever in any danger from an errant bullet.

Directions: Take Hammonton Smartsville Road, fifteen miles from the Simpson Lane–traffic light, east to Chuck Yeager Road, and turn right. Or from Highway 20 in Smartsville, take Hammonton Smartsville Road, one mile to Chuck Yeager Road, and turn left Take Chuck Yeager Road, 4.0 miles to a locked white metal gate on the left. Park on side of road; do not block the gate.

Walsh Trail (756')   1–4   M   *Blue oak woodland, views*

This is an old wagon road, which mostly follows the fence line along the wildlife area boundary from Chuck Yeager Road to the junction with the Four Ponds Trail. It is fairly unremarkable except for some excellent views of the Sacramento Valley from a side ridge at the trail's midpoint. The large hill rising to the east is Walsh Hill.

Directions: Take Hammonton Smartsville Road, fifteen miles from the Simpson Lane–traffic light, east to Chuck Yeager Road, and turn right. Or from Highway 20 in Smartsville, take Hammonton Smartsville Road, one mile to Chuck Yeager Road, and turn left Take Chuck Yeager Road, 2.3 miles to a locked metal gate on the left; do not block the gate.

Council Rocks (800')   1   E   *Large rock outcrops, blue oak woodland*

This is the greatest group of rock outcrops at Spenceville, easily the most picturesque section of the wildlife area after Fairy Falls and the most challenging to access. There are no gates to clamber over, unless one parks at the mailboxes on Daugherty Road, climbs the gate there, and ascends the southern flank of Rose Hill to drop down the far side of the ridge.

Climb over the metal stile at the barbed-wire fence at the pull-out on Chuck Yeager Road and follow the rock outcrops that ring the meadow. There is no trail, not even a cow or coyote path, but grass doesn't grow well in granitic soil; so if you beeline it to the next visible rock, you will find the path of least resistance, always heading for the large boulder in the north end of the meadow. From this boulder, head northeast to the draw, where a small creek runs in winter. At the creek, you can find a path that heads across and up to the immense granite outcrops, which begin to emerge among the trees. One can spend hours wandering here, where within just a few acres, there are rows of outcrops that dwarf those at Rock City a few miles to the north.

Directions: Take Hammonton Smartsville Road, fifteen miles from the Simpson Lane–traffic light, east to Chuck Yeager Road, and turn right. Or from Highway 20 in Smartsville, take Hammonton Smartsville Road, one mile to Chuck Yeager Road, and turn left Take Chuck Yeager Road, 1.8 miles to a large pullout on the right.

Rose Hill (1056')   3   M   *Blue oak woodland, views, pine hollow*

There are great views to be found here, plus rock outcrops and real single-person trails, probably courtesy of the cows that roam here in winter. Rose Hill is the long ridge west of Chuck Yeager Road from Hammonton Smartsville Road to the Council Rocks. It is possible to reach the trails along the ridgeline of Rose Hill directly from the gate across from the Daugherty Road mailboxes, but it is much more scenic and interesting to take the trail up through the Council Rocks area, taking a visible path that skirts the corner fence-line and heads up the ridge in a brief climb to the top and over to a clear trail, which passes through a woodland at the top of a gray pine hollow, the largest such hollow throughout Spenceville.

At the trail junction, take the uphill path over the crest of the hill, which offers views to the east. This is the only area at Spenceville from which the Sierra Buttes are visible, as well as the rooftops of Smartsville. The trail, which has been following an old wagon road, ends at a fence-line. In returning, follow the trail along the rim of the west side of Rose Hill, with excellent views of the Sutter Buttes and Coast Range and of the pine hollow below. Rock outcrops jut from the rim and provide good sitting spots to enjoy the view.

Directions: Take Hammonton Smartsville Road, fifteen miles from the Simpson Lane–traffic light, east to Chuck Yeager Road, and turn right. Or from Highway 20 in Smartsville, take Hammonton Smartsville Road, one mile to Chuck Yeager Road, and turn left. Take Chuck Yeager Road, 1.8 miles to a large pullout on the right. To access Rose Hill directly, take Chuck Yeager Road, 0.9 miles, and park at the mailboxes on Daugherty Road across from the locked green metal gate.

Rock City (651') 3 M *Large rock outcrops, blue oak woodland, views*

This is a separate unit of Spenceville located on Hammonton Smartsville Road at the edge of the foothills. Beyond the gate, it's a short ascent on the old ranch road (right at the fork about fifty yards from the trailhead) to the ridge lined with rock outcrops, some impressively huge like small citadels. There is an excellent view of the valley and the Sutter Buttes from the ridge, making this a prime spot to watch the sunset. From an outcrop of pink granite at the north boundary of the unit, the Highway 20 bridge across the Yuba River is visible.

Directions: Take Hammonton Smartsville Road, 12.3 miles from Simpson Lane, to a locked green metal gate on the left. From Highway 20 in Smartsville, it is 3.7 miles to the gate. Park on either side of the road; do not block the gate.

Black Swan Preserve
Black Swan Trail (1000')   2   M   *Blue oak woodland, views, scenic pond*

This is a delightful and unexpectedly scenic path. Best done clockwise, the trailhead for the loop is clearly marked at the parking area. It gradually winds up through thick brush (watch for poison oak) and then an open hillside to an old ditch path. The flat path allows for a slow stroll, shaded by blue oaks as the views expand of the nearby foothills. Huge Black Swan Pond, with its islands and peninsulas, comes into view. After circling around above the pond, a newer path leaves the ditch and cuts down to the right, connecting to an old road that drops in a long half mile to the pond. As one approaches the pond, it is impossible to miss the sheer escarpment towering over; it is jaw-dropping to realize that you were just walking along the top of that escarpment. After pausing to enjoy the quiet of the pond, and the multitude of birds it attracts, continue around the pond and follow the old road a half mile to the parking area.

Directions: Take Highway 20 to the Yuba–Nevada county line and turn north on Mooney Flat Road. The signed parking area for Black Swan Preserve is on the left, approximately 0.25 mile from Highway 20.

Deer Creek Narrows (800')   3.5   M   *Blue oak woodland, creek gorge*

Just above its confluence with the Yuba River near the Yuba Narrows, Deer Creek drops through its own scenic narrows. To access this bit of foothill landscape drama, take the old access road from the metal gate below the parking area to Black Swan Pond and head north on the old road. Where the Black Swan Trail descends from its upper leg, continue straight ahead past it. The old road allows for a pleasant stroll through the foothill woodland. Where the route curves to the left and begins to head west, look for an old trail that continues north across a meadow. Where this path ends at an oak grove, look for an obvious path that cuts down the slope through the trees. The path is steep, but only briefly. You emerge on a ledge with a full view of Deer Creek's rocky narrows, upstream and down toward the Yuba River. Actual creek access is possible only after some gymnastic scrambling, so for most people, a good plan is to enjoy the dramatic view and then return. In the future, an improved trail might provide less adventurous access, and the view will still be grand.

Directions: Take Highway 20 to the Yuba–Nevada county line and turn north on Mooney Flat Road. The signed parking area for Black Swan Preserve is on the left, approximately 0.25 mile from Highway 20.

Daugherty Hill Wildlife Area—Three separate units comprise this wildlife area.
Daugherty Hill (504') 2 M *Blue oak woodland, view of Collins Lake*

From the parking area, open meadows span out. In nearby marshy McGinn Creek, frogs croak away. A footpath leaves the parking area and connects shortly with a maintenance road. Turn right on the road and ascend gradually toward the wooded hillside. Double-peaked Daugherty Hill, 1,790 feet high, rises to the southeast. Upon reaching the ditch, turn right and follow the ditch path through a gate and into a narrow canyon. For about one hundred yards, the route is directly under power lines. Paralleling the power lines, the road climbs to a gap in the ridge. Just before the road drops to Dry Creek, the trace of an old spur road takes off to the right. Follow this spur not too far for a view of Collins Lake. Return to your vehicle the way you came. Note: there are no roads or trails to the summit of

Daugherty Hill. One may bushwhack up the thickly wooded slopes, but ticks and poison oak are ubiquitous.

Directions: Take Marysville Road from Highway 20 in Browns Valley three miles to Dolan Harding / Peoria Road and turn right. After Peoria Road cuts away, Dolan Harding Road is unpaved but well-graded. The parking area is on the right, a half mile after encountering the yellow metal plates on the fence, which denote the wildlife area.

Donovan Hill (1630')   3   M/SC   *Blue oak woodland, views*

Donovan Hill is a mile-long ridge offering tremendous views of the Sacramento Valley. Walk through fence opening, cross the fire break, and follow the unsigned trail uphill. The trail, a former ranch road, is about a mile from start to top. As the trail climbs, the views become expansive. Stanfield Hill rises to the east, and Daugherty Hill fills the southeast horizon. Near the top, look east for a glimpse of Collins Lake. At the top, turn right on the old road and leisurely follow it to a parklike meadow at the northern end of the ridge. From the ridgetop, there is an excellent view of the Sacramento Valley, Sutter Buttes, Coast Range (including Snow Mountain and the Yolla Bolly Mountains), downtown Sacramento, and even Mt Diablo like a distant sentinel. Paynes Peak's craggy knob rises among the Loma Rica ranches. Return the way you came.

Directions: Take Marysville Road from Highway 20 in Browns Valley, seven miles to Loma Rica Road. Turn left, and in one hundred feet, look for a parking area on the right side of Loma Rica Road.

Honcut Creek (900')   1   E   *Honcut Creek, foothill valley, foothill woodland*

Formally a separate unit of Daugherty Hill Wildlife Area, this area straddles Honcut Creek in a deep foothill valley. Though not offering extensive hikes, it is pleasant for short strolls on old paths and roads. In autumn, when the little valley fills with the golden hues of the season, it is reminiscent of a "cove," those hidden vales tucked into the Great Smoky Mountains. A small, rocky narrows in Honcut Creek sits downstream from where Darby Road crosses the creek, just past the wildlife area entrance.

Directions: From Highway 70 in south Butte County, turn right on Lower Honcut Road. Proceed through the small community of Honcut to where Ramirez Road comes in from the right, and you veer left on what is now La Porte Road. In Bangor, continue through the small community on La Porte Road, three miles to Darby Road. Turn right on Darby to the end of the road, where there is a signed entrance to the wildlife area. Follow the narrow unpaved road a quarter mile to a parking area. To reach the creek narrows, bypass the entrance a short distance and park just past the creek. A 0.25-mile trail heads downstream.

Lake Oroville (901')   2.5   E   *Lake view, foothill woodland*

The 0.2-mile Chaparral Trail, just below the visitor center, is an easy loop through the foothill plant community, primarily blue oaks, gray pines, and manzanita. The Dan Beebe Trail, just past the Chaparral Trail, begins with a junction. To the left, Oroville Dam is 0.9 mile. Take the choice to the right, 1.2 miles to Kelly Ridge Point. The trail is packed earth, broad and well-graded. At first level, the trail gradually drops along the ridge, with peeks of surrounding ridges through the mature oaks, pines, and manzanita.

At the junction with Bidwell Canyon Trail, take the left fork. Bits of the blue lake become visible through the trees. At a four-way junction, turn left on the Kelly Ridge Trail and wind down to a wooded point overlooking the broad lake. A wooden picnic table provides an excellent view of the lake's three branches of the Feather River. To the east, beyond the houseboat marina, is Bidwell Bridge, like a miniature Golden Gate Bridge straddling the Middle Fork. Two miles up that branch is the boating access for views of Feather Falls, sixth highest waterfall in the US, visible up Falls River Canyon.

Directly west of the point is the dam, site of the February 2017 spillway failure, which led to evacuation of all downstream communities. Return to the four-way junction and continue to the visitor center straight ahead on the Kelly Ridge Trail. It is a moderate uphill climb to the junction with the Dan Beebe Trail. Take the righthand choice, as the trail crests the ridge and levels out. The visitor center sits in an attractive wooded area on top of the ridge. There is an excellent museum regarding the history of the area, including construction of the dam. A forty-seven-foot tower (stairs only) offers a panoramic view of the lake and the surrounding foothills.

Directions: From Highway 70 in Oroville, take Highway 162 (Oro Dam Blvd) east for 7.1 miles and turn left onto Kelly Ridge Road. Follow Kelly Ridge Road, 2.3 miles to the visitor center.

North Table Mountain (1320')　1–6　M　*Rare wildflowers, waterfalls, views, woodland hollows*

Visible for miles across the valley, this lava plateau appears flat and treeless. Rolling landscape up close, it is not a table as much as shelves of ancient lava. From March into May, this ecological preserve is a wildflower wonderland. It then looks like a multicolored carpet in all directions, our own natural Hanging Gardens of Babylon (one of the original Seven Wonders of the World). There are plants here found nowhere else on the planet. Vernal pools gather in shallow pockets across the landscape. Picturesque waterfalls flow from the lower rims. In late spring, flowers are fewer, when smatterings of lupine fade into the goldening grass. Out in the valley, the Sutter Buttes and Coast Range jaggedly mark the horizon.

There are few designated trails here. The most popular path drops from the parking area and follows a seasonal creek less than a mile to the rim where Hollow Falls drops fifty feet into wooded Beatson Hollow. Near the top of the falls, a narrow path threads down into the hollow. From the bottom of the falls, a pleasant trail wanders through a verdant oak and poison oak-filled woodland.

About halfway between the parking area and Hollow Falls, at a small grove of large oaks, a wide path cuts off to the right. With a round trip of 4.2 miles, this trail takes a relatively direct route to a postcard-perfect view of seasonal 165-foot Phantom Falls dropping ribbonlike into spectacular Coal Canyon. Along the way, the trail passes a small hollow, the top of which provides a scenic rest where unseen Ravine Falls and a companion waterfall flow into the rocky chasm. Please note that on the entire route to Phantom Falls, there is no shade except for the viewpoint at the end of the trail, which on warm days makes this trail best at sunrise. Explore the top of Phantom Falls at your own risk. The drop is vertical and provides no view of the waterfall.

If wandering free-form over the landscape anywhere on North Table Mountain, be careful to note the huge lone oak by the parking area for your return to the trailhead. The seasonal creeks have cut deep ravines into the tabletop, and it is easy to become disoriented.

During wildflower season, this is an exceptionally popular place. Avoid the weekend hordes and arrive early to secure a parking place. Porta-potties are provided at this time; otherwise, there are no restroom facilities, drinking water, or trash receptacles. A California Land-Use Pass is required for each visitor to the preserve.

Directions: Take Highway 70 to Grand Ave in Oroville, exit and head east on Grand Avenue. At Table Mountain Boulevard, turn left and at the new round-about, turn right onto Cherokee Road. Turn right onto Cherokee Road. After seven miles of winding up onto flat-topped Table Mountain, park in the parking area on the left.

(Note: Access to Phantom Falls is no longer available beyond the fence-line above Ravine Falls.)

Paradise Ridge—More than one ridge is involved here, but this section covers the trails along Skyway from Paradise through Magalia to Stirling City. Named after a stage stop, a saloon named Pair-O-Dice, Paradise Ridge, is bound by deep canyons, West Branch Feather River east and Butte Creek to the west. A residentially settled dense pine forest extends between the canyon rims across a rolling terrain.

Bille Park (2050') 0.5 M *Hillside grotto, view of Butte Creek canyon*

This is a former olive-and-grape ranch. To serve the mines, farming was prevalent along the ridge. Before the miners, Maidu lived here. The short but scenic trail to Lookout Point starts below the pavilion at the north end of the park. It is rare to be alone on this trail. At the beginning of the trail is a short side trail to the Grotto, a hillside cove of moss and ferns.

The geology of the ridge is a lava cap, and here water has broken through, dripping down the canyon wall. A deck and bench provide a restful place to enjoy the lush surroundings and idyllic view of Butte Creek Canyon. At the junction of the Grotto and main trails are Maidu grinding holes. The Lookout Point Trail continues unpaved, and after passing through, laurel trees emerge on the open lava cap. A bench sits at trail's end with an expansive view of the canyon. In spring, blue lupine covers the slope. Dogs are permitted on leash.

Directions: From Highway 99 in Chico, take Skyway to Bille Road in Paradise. Turn left and follow Bille Road to the park's main entrance. To park closer to the trail, follow the signs from Bille Road to the north entrance on Wagstaff.

Upper Ridge Preserve (2300') 0.25–5 E *Forest trails, view of Butte Creek canyon*

120 acres of numerous paths wind through a dense, mixed-growth woodscape over a moderately flat terrain. At the western edge of the preserve, near the Ponderosa Way entrance, there is a bench at a vista point overlooking Butte Creek Canyon. By continuing down the closed portion of Ponderosa, it is possible to connect with the creek-side trail into the Magalia Greenbelt. Dogs are permitted on leash.

Directions: From Highway 99 in Chico, take Skyway Road through Paradise into Magalia. Past Magalia Reservoir, turn left on Ponderosa Way. There are two entrances. For the first, turn left from Ponderosa onto Compton and soon arrive at a gravel road on the right with a locked metal gate. Park so as not to block the gate. The second entrance is another locked gate at the end of Ponderosa. Again, do not block the gate.

Magalia Greenbelt (2460')   1–3   M   *Forested canyon, Lil Falls*

This offers a pleasant stroll in a quiet, heavily forested canyon. Look for the wooden sign nailed to a tree. Drop down onto the trail from Colter. The first one hundred feet follows the creek past backyards. Then the backyards and the dull rumble of Skyway fall away, and the path becomes an old, flat logging road. At about a half mile, Lower Trail cuts down to the left. This will be the return route of a loop to Lil Falls. Continue on Upper Trail for a nice view of the canyon.

At a trail on the left with a sign for Lil Falls, drop into the canyon on switchbacks to Lower Trail alongside the creek. Lil Falls, unseen, is directly below the trail junction, and its "li'l" roar is audible. Turn right and follow Lower Trail downstream, a short distance to the signed side trail for Lil Falls. The falls are aptly named. After visiting the falls, return to Lower Trail and turn right for a pretty creek-side walk. (Turn left, and it is possible to reach Ponderosa Way in a few miles and connect to Upper Ridge Preserve.) The trail reaches open slopes and climbs out of the canyon. In spring, the rocky slope is covered with wildflowers. Lower Trail connects with Upper Trail and the return to the trailhead. Dogs are permitted on leash.

Directions: From Highway 99 in Chico, take Skyway Road through Paradise into Magalia. Turn left on Colter Way (2.4 miles past Ponderosa Way). Immediately turn left on Masterson Way and park, being respectful that this is a residential street. The trailhead for Upper Trail is on Colter, where Middle Butte Creek flows under the road.

Clotilde Merlo Park (3570')   1   E   *Landscaped ponds, statues, forest trails, historic site*

Here the site of a former mill-town enclave known as "Little Italy" has been transformed into a mostly manicured park. Strolling paths wind among a large variety of trees and manmade ponds. Whimsical statues of children at play are scattered throughout the park. For a stroll in the eastern "wild" area, the Varbenaga Trail begins near the end of the upper footbridge. It's a wide gravel path that enters the woods behind the chapel. Shortly you reach a junction with a maze of trails through a quiet second-growth woodland of pines, firs, incense cedars, dogwoods, and maples. The trails are narrow, old roads, thickly carpeted with pine needles. Dogs are not permitted. Open May–October, Thursday through Sunday.

Directions: From Highway 99 in Chico, take Skyway Road through Paradise and Magalia to Stirling City. In Stirling City, turn right on Retson Road, and in one-third mile, find the entrance and parking area for the park.

Bidwell Park, Chico—This is one of the largest municipal parks in the country and, in any other state, would be a major draw. The park extends eleven miles from downtown Chico into the foothills.

Lower Bidwell Park (197') 1–5 E Valley oak woodland, Big Chico Creek

Though technically in the valley, Lower Bidwell Park is included here because of its connection with the foothills through Upper Bidwell. Flat paths on both sides of Big Chico Creek thread through the most sylvan wood scape in the valley. Though heavily used, quiet, shady nooks along the creek—many with tables—provide a sense of solitude. Lower Bidwell stood in for Sherwood Forest during filming of the Errol Flynn, *Adventures of Robin Hood*. Dogs are permitted on leash.

Directions: From the Highway 32, exit from Highway 99, head east, and immediately turn left, following signs for Bidwell Park. Turn right on E Eighth Street and follow it to the park entrance on the left just past Kern Street. If the entry gate is closed, park at the Chico Creek Nature Center just beyond.

Upper Bidwell Park, Chico
Monkeyface Rock (550') 2–5 M *Rim access, rocky viewpoint*

All trails are well signed here. From the trailhead at the Horseshoe Lake parking area, Monkeyface Rock is the promontory on the rim above. It is easily identifiable because it is likely that members of your fellow species will be moving about on top of it. The rocky point is so named because of its resemblance to the profile of a chimpanzee hunkered against the rim, but it could also apply to all those scrambling monkeylike over the rock's crown. It is fairly easy to access. A mazelike network of trails branch out in pretty much every direction, but just keep your eye on the rock at every junction and choose the trail heading most directly to the rock. Up on the rim, you'll have easy access to the rock and to North Rim Trail. Regardless of how energetic you feel, the view of the Chico Creek canyon expanding is always splendid.

Directions: Take East Avenue exit from Highway 99 in north Chico and head east on East Avenue to the roundabout at Manzanita Avenue and the entrance to Upper Bidwell. Follow the park road a few miles into the park to the Horseshoe Lake parking area at the end of the paved portion of the park road.

North Rim Loop (1,263') 4 M/SC *Rim walk, views, Chico Creek gorge*

Among the many trail options here, the loop along the North Rim and then back along the creekside, Yahi Trail, offers the best of the rugged upper park. From the Bear Hole parking area, cross the park road and follow a used path to access Middle Trail, which parallels the road. Turn right on Middle Trail, a short distance to the junction with Upper Trail. Take Upper Trail a short distance and turn right on Live Oak Trail (unmarked). Live Oak Trail climbs the canyon (it's as steep as it looks, but it's a brief ascent) to the North Rim Trail.

Turn right and follow the trail, pausing to take in the spectacular vista. Sometimes you will need to venture away from the main trail for a better view. Descend on the "B" Trail and return to Bear Hole on the Yahi Trail, which follows Little Chico Creek at the edge of its scenic inner gorge. Dogs are permitted off-leash north of the park road. A word of caution to dog owners: the biggest bobcat I've ever seen bounded across my path twenty feet in front of me on the Yahi Trail. Mountain lions have also been sighted in Upper Park, tracking the deer herds, which are frequently seen.

Directions: Take East Avenue exit from Highway 99 in north Chico and head east on East Avenue to the roundabout at Manzanita Avenue and the entrance to Upper Bidwell. Follow the park road a few miles into the park and past the iron gate (open Friday and Saturday only), onto the unpaved section of road. Park at Bear Hole.

South Rim Trails (1215')   3–5   M   *Foothill woodland, views*

As the name suggests, part of this network of paths threads along a bluff below the igneous palisades of the South Rim. The area of Bidwell Park south of Chico Creek is devoid of hikers, relative to the hordes that flock to the trails north of the creek. This is due to the lack of a bridge across the creek other than at the golf course near the entrance to Upper Bidwell. Even if you're sharing the South Rim trails, it's likely you will see no trace of anyone else except their vehicle at the trailhead.

The trail begins by winding around the gate and then descends immediately on old 10-Mile House Road. Just beyond the first bend is the junction with the Guardians Trail on your left. For a loop, continue on down 10 Mile House Road, 1.2 miles to the junction with the Annie Bidwell Trail (ABT). Take the ABT one mile to the steep Bloody Pins Trail for a climb of just less than a mile to the Guardians Trail. You can continue along this view-filled trail back to 10 Mile House Road, or turn right and head to the disc golf course if you have a shuttle waiting. The Guardians Trail extends for 3.4 miles along the South Rim palisades. An additional option is to stay on the ABT, which meanders for 4.7 uncrowded miles along the south rim of Chico Creek's inner gorge, again with a shuttle waiting.

Directions: Take Highway 32 east from Highway 99 in Chico for ten miles. Look for a large pullout on the left next to an old road with a locked gate.

Upper Foothills—*This is the region between the sunbaked lower elevations and the rugged high country of the Sierra Nevada. More densely vegetated than the predominant mix of blue oaks, live oaks, and gray pines found lower, summer days are generally cooler and snow is rare in winter.*

Stevens Creek Falls, Colfax

Grass Valley
Adam Ryan Wildlife Preserve
Alan Thiesen Trail
Empire Mine State Historic Park
Hard Rock Trail
Union Hill Loop

Nevada City
Deer Creek Tribute Trail
Hirschman Pond
Woodpecker Wildlife Preserve
Orene Wetherall Trail

South Yuba River State Park
Bridgeport
Pt. Defiance Loop
Buttermilk Bend
Independence Trail

Rice's Crossing Preserve
Yuba Rim Trail

Pioneer Trail
Rock Creek Nature Trail

Malakoff Diggins State Historic Park
Diggins Trail
Humbug Trail

Feather Falls

Bald Rock
Bald Dome Trail

Bald Rock

Stevens Creek Falls, Colfax (2,425') 3–12 M View of North American River canyon, seasonal waterfall

The Stevens Trail is an old road that connected Colfax with Indian Hill. The intrepid hiker can manage to conquer the full twelve-mile round-trip to the river and back up out of the river canyon in one day, but most are happy with the first 1.5 miles to the seasonal waterfall. The trail immediately drops away from the trailhead. I-80, above to the left, is unseen but very audible.

After about 0.25 miles, the highway becomes a dull rumble and then fades away altogether, leaving you to descend the broad, shaded path accompanied by birdsong and the rustle of breezes. Poison oak is thick along the trail. Creeklets small enough to step over trickle across the path. After the third creeklet, the trail levels off and follows the contour along the slope. After crossing a plank footbridge, you reach a junction with another old road and turn right. The trail climbs here with little shade, but after it crests the spur ridge, it drops soon to another trail junction. Take this trail on the left, and you're back to single-track width and shade.

At the next junction, the Stevens Trail splits. Motorized vehicles head downhill on the right; hikers take the more even left path. Soon a large rock outcrop is visible ahead, like a sentinel over the emerging-into-view North Fork American River Canyon. When flowing, Stevens Creek Falls is now audible ahead. Best viewed from the rock outcrop, the waterfall has an impressive one-hundred-foot drop that decreases to a trickle by late spring. For those continuing on, it is another three miles to the river.

Directions: The well-marked trailhead, with parking and a restroom, is located in Colfax at the eastern end of Canyon Way, which is the frontage road along the south side of I-80.

Grass Valley—There are a number of walking paths in the Grass Valley–area. Mostly used by locals, the trails offer peace.

Adam Ryan Nature Preserve
Alan Thiesen Trail (2,310')   1.5   M   *Foothill oak woods*

The preserve is forty acres, but feels larger. From the parking area, a maintenance road plows unimaginatively up the hill. At the base of the hill, a footpath extends left and right. Take the right path, and the loop will return on the left. Ascending into a grove of young ponderosa pines, Alta Sierra Road becomes obscured, and only the occasional vehicle reminds you of the road's presence. A grove of young cedars was sprung from seeds deposited by birds.

After these shady groves, the trail emerges into a small meadow bordering on a neighborhood, with paths cutting off toward the nearest homes. Bear left and continue on the broad trail, continuing to ascend to the crest of the hill. Stay on the designated trail and allow traces of old paths return to nature. From the crest, the country-club golf course is visible to the west. The trail passes oaks and a huge madrone tree.

Please refrain from scrambling up the tangled limbs in order not to damage the bark or weaken the roots. The true crown of the hill is safely removed from errant golf balls and vehicle noise. It is a pleasant spot to pause and savor the sounds of birdsong and the breeze rustling the leaves. From here the trail begins its descent down the manzanita-dominated eastern flanks of the hill. The trail contours down to the Rattlesnake Ditch, and the route becomes the old ditch-tender's path. Use caution with children because the ditch is usually running with murky water. Ignore the downhill-plunging maintenance road and take the next single-track path that cuts down to the left.

At the next junction, where a gravel road bears to the right, take the single-track path to the left. After crossing a series of small meadows, the final portion of the loop is parallel with Dog Bar Road, though the thick brush blocks any actual view of traffic. Dogs are permitted on leash.

Directions: Located five miles south of Grass Valley, take Auburn Street south from downtown Grass Valley. It briefly becomes La Barr Meadow Road before turning into Dog Bar Road. The small parking area is at the southwest corner of Dog Bar and Alta Sierra Roads.

Empire Mine State Park
Hard Rock Trail (2500')   1–5   E   *Foothill oak-fir forest, old mining sites*

From the Pennsylvania Gate trailhead, follow the old mining road past mining sites. At the WYOD (Work Your Own Diggins) side trails, kids of all ages will enjoy running up and down the hillocks created by mining. The main trail crosses Little Wolf Creek and winds around through a second growth oak-fir woodland to the main park buildings, circumnavigating the Exclusion Area, a toxic waste site from mining days, for which warning signs are amply displayed. It's not noticeable because the forest has grown enough to hide the no-man's-land. As the trail circles around, it passes the junction with the Osborn Hill trails, which loop through former mining sites. Arriving at the visitor center, one can pay the nominal fee and tour the mine and its grounds. To return to the Penn Gate, it is possible to make a loop along the busy street-side path, but it is probably more pleasant to retrace your steps. Dogs are permitted on leash.

Directions: Take Highway 20 to Grass Valley. At Highway 49, instead of turning onto 49, cross the freeway. Follow Empire Street, which Highway 20 becomes, to the state park. The Pennsylvania Gate trailhead (parking is free) is located on Empire Street at the edge of the park, a mile before the main entrance.

Union Hill Loop (2500')   2.25   E   *Dense mixed fir-oak forest*

From the trailhead, follow the Indian Ridge Trail, an old logging road, on a gradual uphill grade through a dense fir forest, much thicker than other nearby woodlands. Pass the Pipeline Trail and turn left on the Upper Union Trail, which drops down and makes a pleasant loop to the trailhead. The dense cedar forest, cool and green, always seems like the perfect location for a film version of *Hansel and Gretel.* There are rarely many people on the Union Hill–trails. Dogs are permitted on leash.

Directions: In Grass Valley, from Colfax Avenue (Highway 174), turn onto Gold Hill Road across from Memorial Park, just before Highway 174 climbs out of town. Follow Gold Hill Road up to its end at the small trailhead parking.

Nevada City—Late in providing walking opportunities outside of its historic downtown, there are now a couple of appealing options for walkers.

Deer Creek Tribute Trail (2,400')   0.5–11   E   *Foothill oak woods, Deer Creek, Nevada City*

The eastern portion of the trail is really a route along historic Nevada City streets, traffic included, except for the wooded shortcut above Little Deer Creek from the Pioneer Park trailhead to downtown Nevada City. The "real" trail, away from cars and asphalt, begins on Old Downieville Highway at the junction with Champion Mine Road.

Hirschman Pond (2,663')   0.5–4   E   *Foothill woodland, scenic pond*

From the parking area, it's less than a half-mile to the pond on a broad, flat, old quarry road. The path and pond are very scenic, with picturesque granite outcrops along the way. Highway 49 is not far away but rarely intrudes with any rumble of traffic. In winter, seasonal wetlands add a marshy quality to the surrounding woods, providing unique opportunities for forest reflections. The pond itself, with its hydraulically sculpted bluffs, is exceptionally pretty, with a jumble of boulders along the south shore, where it is easy to scramble off the trail for a better view of the pond. A bench sits pleasantly pondside at its western edge, near a gold rush–era water cannon. Beyond the pond, it is one mile through dense woods—often near

Highway 49—to Woods Ravine Trail, and two miles to the western terminus.

Directions: From Nevada City, travel west on northbound Highway 49 to Cement Hill Road, just past the county government center. Turn right on Cement Hill Road for about fifty feet to the parking area on the left, signed for Hirschman Pond.

Woodpecker Wildlife Preserve
Orene Wetherall Trail (3,200') 1-5   3.2   E/M   *Mixed oak-conifer forest, Cascade Canal, Woodpecker Preserve*

Access to this loop is via the Cascade Canal Trail. From Gracie Road, this flat ditch-tender's path extends 5.0 miles to Red Dog Road. The rise in elevation as you proceed is very gradual and imperceptible. Through breaks in the dense forest, there are expansive views of Nevada City and Harmony Ridge. The Woodpecker Wildlife Preserve adjoins the trail on the north. The Orene Wetherall Trail, named for the wife of the donor of the preserve's land, cuts downhill into the twenty-eight-acre preserve. After completing the loop, retrace your steps to the Cascade Canal Trail and then to Gracie Road.

From Highway 49 in Grass Valley, take the Brunswick exit. Go west and turn right on E. Main Street. Travel to Banner Lava Cap Road. Turn right and travel to Gracie Road. Turn left. The parking area is seven hundred feet downhill from the intersection with Banner Lava Cap Road. The signed trailhead is on Gracie Road.

South Yuba River State Park
Bridgeport (563') 0.25–1   E   *Covered bridge, easy access*

Besides the covered bridge, justly notable for being the longest bridge of its type, there are short, easy paths for the casual walker. Options around Bridgeport include the tiny cemetery south of the visitor center, and the old resort road to Kneebone Beach. That pleasant riverside area is the site of a former resort, which was here in the early twentieth century.

Directions to Bridgeport: Take Pleasant Valley Road from Highway 20 in Penn Valley, past Lake Wildwood, and then descend to the river in South Fork Yuba River State Park.

Point Defiance Loop (590')   2.5   M   *Foothill woodland, Englebright Lake*

Across from the parking area on the north side of the river, the trail climbs over a shallow ridge and descends on a maintenance road with continuous views of Englebright Lake to Point Defiance, where picnic tables are found. The loop trail returns along the South Yuba River to the covered bridge.

Directions: See directions to Bridgeport above.

Buttermilk Bend (567')   2.5   E   *South Yuba River, wildflowers (spring), dogs on leash*

Following an old railroad bed, the path is flat with constant views of the river. The trail ends at a landslide, and it is necessary to retrace your steps; but just before trail's end, there is easy access to the river. Wildflower viewing in springtime is so excellent here identification signs are placed along the trail.

Directions: See directions to Bridgeport above.

Independence Trail (1,450')   2–9   E   *Mixed fir-oak woodland, waterfall, view of South Yuba River, dogs on leash*

A reclaimed gold rush–flume, this was the first official trail for the handicapped. Now a pleasantly level path, it offers pleasant views of the South Yuba canyon. The eastern section extends 2.5 miles, and the western section two miles from Highway 49. A mile west of Highway 49, Rush Creek Falls is accessible via plank ramps. Beyond Rush Creek, a four-mile loop is possible by backtracking via Jones Bar on the river.

Directions: Take Highway 49 north from Nevada City (really west at the point where the highway leaves the town) to just inside the South Yuba River State Park boundary. Park alongside the road. If you reach the river, you've gone too far.

Rice's Crossing Preserve
Yuba Rim Trail (3,000')   4.5   M   *Forested ridge, view of Yuba River Canyon*

For most of this hike, there is no view. Indeed, one of the best views of the Yuba River canyon is from the trailhead. The other option for long-range scenery is the designated viewpoint, which looks down at the confluence of the middle and north forks of the Yuba River.

The trail drops from the trailhead to a meadow along the canyon rim. Instead of crossing that meadow, the trail makes a sharp right. Watch for the sign. The single-track path, relatively newly constructed, skirts the meadow and threads through the surrounding forest. At about one mile, the trail crosses a footbridge and climbs in a few, short switchbacks to a former logging road. As the forest grows upon it, the old road is gradually evolving into a single-track path. The trail follows the ridge crest, but dense foliage on both sides prohibit any views until the vista point at the end of a spur ridge. Eventually, the Yuba Rim Trail will extend south down the Yuba River canyon and connect with Bridgeport at South Yuba River State Park.

Directions: The signed trailhead is on Marysville Road, twelve miles east of Dobbins and three miles west of Bullards Bar Dam. There is little room for vehicles at the trailhead pullout and more parking across the road in the old quarry. There are no restrooms or water at the trailhead.

Pioneer Trail (3,500')   0.25–25   E   *Midmountain forest, historical route*

The historic Pioneer Trail extends from Five Mile House, seven miles east of Nevada City, on the route of the 1850 cutoff on the Emigrant Trail, paralleling Highway 20. There are many access points along the highway. From White Cloud Campground, the trail can be taken through dense forest to the Washington Overlook, with its expansive view of the South Yuba River canyon and the rugged Sierra Buttes about ten miles north. At the Omega Overlook, a 0.25-mile paved trail heads west to an observation deck, which looks into the South Yuba River canyon, with the Omega Mine below and the numerous pink telltale traces of past mining operations across forested ridges. The scenic section of the Pioneer Trail near Spaulding Reservoir is covered elsewhere here in an entry under that title.

Rock Creek Nature Trail (2,900') 0.75 E *Second-growth, canyon-bottom forest, historical site, good for kids*

This is an easy loop on the site of a lumber mill that operated from 1879–94. Interpretive signs provide some forest education. The little valley here was clear-cut for the mill, but the forest has densely reclaimed the area. Here can be found a mountain mix of dogwood, hazelnut, big-leaf maple, madrone, black oak, ponderosa pine, Douglas fir, incense cedar, and, in the shadows, white fir. The loop is entirely flat and pleasantly shaded. Half of its length is along babbling Rock Creek, which flows into Lake Vera and then on to the South Yuba River.

Directions: From the junction of Highways 49 and 20 in Nevada City, it is 6.9 miles east on Highway 20 to the left turn signed for Washington Ridge Conservation Camp. After one mile on this paved, gradually descending road, turn left on an unpaved road signed for Rock Creek. This unpaved but well-graded road drops down for a mile and is not recommended in wet weather. At the trailhead, there is a small parking area, picnic tables and a restroom.

From here, you can choose to return to Highway 20 at Five Mile House on a two-mile one-way road.

Malakoff Diggins State Historic Park
Diggins Trail (3,080')   0.5–4   E   *Pine-fir forest, historical site, colorful formations*

One might think they've somehow passed through an invisible portal on this hike and landed somewhere in Southern Utah. Though a remnant of reckless hydraulic mining practices in the late 1800s, leaving horrific scars on the terrain, nature has reclaimed the landscape. The Diggins Trail is a 2.78-mile loop accessible from three trailheads along North Bloomfield Road, a trailhead at the old church, and from the visitor center in the historic town of North Bloomfield, which adds a half mile in each direction to the loop.

The loop is mostly level with minimal uphill activity and can be satisfactorily walked in either direction. The northside trail meanders along the base of the bluffs, which tower overhead like pink and buff-colored turrets. Up close, the effect is astonishing in the same way that the colorful pinnacles and hoodoos of the Southwest transfix visitors with an awe that can't be named. The southside portion of the loop, easily accessed from North Bloomfield Road, offers near-continuous views across the Diggins to the pastel escarpment. This is a highly recommended hike in spite of the Diggins in all actuality being a monument to man's damage to our planet.

Directions: From Highway 49 between South Yuba River State Park and south of the historic hamlet of North San Juan, take Tyler Foote Crossing Road east for seventeen miles. Follow the signs for North Bloomfield and Malakoff Diggins because the road changes names to Cruzon Grade and Backbone. For the trailheads closer to the Diggins Loop, continue past North Bloomfield for one mile. A day-use fee is payable at the visitor center in North Bloomfield.

Humbug Trail (3,050') 5.4 M/S *Fir forest, historical site, South Yuba River*

This is a scenic hike to the South Yuba River, but remember, this heads down in various degrees of grades and is an uphill push on the return. A relaxing day by the river is great, but there is a nine-hundred-foot climb. The first mile is a gradual descent through a shaded forest of Douglas fir, cedar, maple, alder, and dogwood. The trail passes three "coyote holes," shafts dug during excavation of the Hiller Tunnel, which drained the Diggins when ponds filled the hydraulic pits. After about a mile, the trail drops into the rocky South Yuba canyon at a steeper rate. Humbug Creek Falls is a horsetail waterfall beside the trail at the 1.5-mile mark. At the river, the Humbug Trail meets the South Yuba Trail, offering easy access in either direction.

Directions: From Highway 49 between South Yuba River State Park and south of the historic hamlet of North San Juan, take Tyler Foote Crossing Road east for seventeen miles. Follow the signs for North Bloomfield and Malakoff Diggins because the road changes names to Cruzon Grade and Backbone. For the trailhead, continue past North Bloomfield for 1.5 miles and look for the trailhead on your left, just past the Hiller Tunnel. A day-use fee is payable at the Visitor Center in North Bloomfield.

Feather Falls (1,942') 9 M/SL *Feather Falls, view of Bald Dome*

The trail is long, if not strenuous, and very popular; so if you seek solitude, look elsewhere. The falls are worth it. At 640 feet, this is the tallest waterfall in the state outside Yosemite. An observation deck perches precipitously on a cliff-side pinnacle, providing an excellent view of the falls and the North Fork Feather River just downstream to the west. (Feather Falls is on Fall Creek.) Along the trail, there are vantage points of Bald Dome to the northwest, where it looms over the North Feather. An old trail takes you to the fenced-off top of the falls and into the shaded canyon of the stream above to the site of an old homestead.

Directions: From Highway 70 in Oroville, take Highway 162, Oro Dam Boulevard, east into the hills. In the hills above Lake Oroville, turn right on Forbestown Road. Turn left on Lumpkin Road for twelve miles to the signed trailhead.

Bald Rock (3,274')   1+   M   *Granite ridge, views*

In any other state, this would be a state park. Here it is only a designated national forest picnic area. Officially, it is Big Bald Rock, with Little Bald Rock and Bald Dome farther north along the ridge. A 0.25-mile easy trail connects the parking area through a dense forest of pines, firs, cedars, and dogwoods to an exceptional two-hundred-acre expanse of smooth granite where you can wander among enormous boulders, like a child among some giant's toys. In the myths of the Maidu, who originally inhabited this area, this was home to a terrible monster named Uino. Vegetation is sparse—manzanita, live oak, pine—all bent by the wind. Expansive views include Lake Oroville, the Sutter Buttes, and the Coast Range. Great for kids, but be vigilant as to where the rounded ledges drop off.

Directions: From Highway 70 in Oroville, take Highway 162, Oro Dam Boulevard, east into the hills. Wind past Lake Oroville—beyond the lake, Highway162 becomes Oroville–Quincy Highway. At the community of Berry Creek, 19.4 miles from Highway 70, turn right on Bald Rock Rd. It is 7.4 miles to the signed parking area on the left, just within Plumas National Forest. The short entry road is rugged but navigable by low-clearance vehicles. There are restrooms, but no picnic tables and no water—the small, seasonal brook is not advisable for drinking.

Bald Dome Trail (2,800')   3   M   *View of Bald Dome, fir forest, North Fork Feather River canyon, Curtain Falls*

From the small parking area, head downhill on the Dome Trail. For 560 yards, the trail is broad, ending at a small granite outcrop. Here the trail narrows and bends to the left into a shady single track. 570 feet down this trail, look for a switchback, which bends sharply to the left. (Missing this turn sends you on the old, unmaintained path that plummets 1.5 miles to the Feather River's Middle Fork at the bottom of Bald Rock Canyon. The small sandy beach at the river is a delight and provides the best views of Bald Dome, but this route is not recommended.)

The correct trail drops in thirty gentle switchbacks to the base of Bald Dome. Along the way, there are three small creeks, which are easily hopped over. Poison oak is profuse along the upper switchbacks. The route across the open face of Bald Dome is fenced for protection, but it is not advisable for small children. The trail culminates at a view of Curtain Falls, a forty-foot drop on the Middle Feather. Popular with kayakers, the river is too swift for swimming. Return the way you came.

Directions: From Highway 70 in Oroville, take Highway 162, Oro Dam Boulevard, east into the hills. Wind past Lake Oroville—beyond the lake, Highway162 becomes Oroville–Quincy Highway. At the community of Berry Creek, turn right on Bald Rock Road. It is 8.7 miles (1.3 miles beyond the Bald Rock parking area) to a crossroad with Zink Road on the left. Turn right on the unnamed road about one mile to the Dome Trail parking area. It is unpaved but appropriate for all vehicles. Near the top of this road, Little Bald Rock is on the right, but on private land and completely obscured by the forest.

Sierra High Country—*This is the snow zone. The foothill woodlands give way to a mixed-fir forest, and the granite landscape becomes more expansive and ruggedly scenic. Predators become scarcer, though bear-crossing signs are now standard on the mountain highways. Neither poison oak nor the smaller foothill rattlesnake is found above five thousand feet, but one should be cautious in a rare encounter with a larger, more aggressive timber rattler.*

Placer Big Trees Grove

Loch Leven Lakes

Donner Summit Area
Mt. Judah
Donner Pass North
Summit Lake
Frog Cliff

Bowman Lake Road Area
Sierra Discovery Trail
Spaulding Lake via Pioneer Trail
Zion Hill
Island Lake
Penner Lake
Grouse Ridge
Downey Lake
Glacier Lake
Loney Meadow

North Yuba River
Canyon Creek Trail
Fiddle Creek Ridge
North Yuba Trail
Halls Ranch Trail
Haypress-Wild Plum Loop
Loves Falls

Sierra Buttes / Lakes Basin
Haskell Peak
Sand Pond Interpretive Loop
Upper Sardine Lake
Mountain Mine Trail
Tamarack Trail
Sierra Buttes
Deer Lake
Lower Salmon Lake
Frazier Falls
Round Lake Loop
Mt. Elwell
Fern Falls
Jamison and Rock Lakes

Bucks Lake Wilderness
Spanish Peak
Gold Lake

Grouse Ridge

Placer Big Trees Grove (5,310') 1.8 E *Northernmost grove of giant sequoias, scary drive*

Located seventy-five miles north of the Calaveras Big Trees, this isolated grove has been suggested to be a separate species of sequoia. It is at the least a relic from the prehistoric past, from a time when these northern Sierra ridges were more hospitable to the immense trees, the monarchs of the forest. The easy 1.8-mile loop through the grove is a pleasant stroll through dense forest, with the towering redwoods providing the cathedral-like aura found in all sequoia groves. With only four old-growth sequoias, it is barely a grove, but there is the same serenity as found in larger groves farther south. The larger Forest View Loop beyond the grove is exactly that—a view of the forest and nothing else. The one caveat to this beautiful spot is that the access via cliff-side Mosquito Ridge Road will be terrifying for anyone who has a problem with heights.

Directions: From I-80 in Auburn, take Foresthill Road and follow the signs to Foresthill. In Foresthill, look for Mosquito Ridge Road on the right. Take Mosquito Ridge Road, 25.5 miles to the signed Big Trees parking area. Mosquito Ridge Road is paved and mostly follows the contours of the mountainside. The first twenty miles hug the cliff, with vertigo-inducing panoramas.

Loch Leven Lakes (6,870') 4 M *Ridgetop scenic lakes, granite expanses, cedar-fir forest*

The easily accessed trailhead means it's a popular place. These are three beautiful lakes perched among on the ruggedly scenic granite expanses atop the ridge between the Yuba and American river watersheds. There are great views into the canyons of each river. The persistent rumble of traffic on I-80 is present during the first two miles as you climb out of the South Yuba canyon, but disappears once you reach the top of the ridge. Quiet Lower Lake is smaller, surrounded by forest. A little farther on, long Middle Lake has a scenic granite escarpment as a backdrop. From the south end of Middle Lake, there is a panoramic view of the North Fork American River canyon. After a mild climb, the trail ends at Upper Lake, situated in a rugged granite basin in true Sierra splendor.

Directions: Take the Cisco Grove exit from I-80, turn left, cross the freeway, turn right on the old highway (historic Route 44) and follow it east to the trailhead along the South Yuba, just past the ranger station.

Donner Summit—This is all about the Sierra Crest and the Pacific Crest Trail. The jaw-dropping views include Mt. Rose in Nevada to the east and the watershed of the South Yuba River to the west.

Mt. Judah (8,049')   4.5   M   *Sierra Crest, Donner Pass, panoramic views*

This is a relatively easy hike to the Sierra crest. From the trailhead, take the Pacific Crest Trail south. For a satisfying loop, pass the first Mt. Judah spur and take the PCT to the Mt. Judah spur at the next gap. As the trail gradually rises, there are broad glimpses of the South Yuba River's upper meadows, through the firs and cedars. It is an easy ascent to the often wind-blasted summit, with spectacular views of the Sierra Crest, Donner Lake, and the Upper South Yuba watershed. Continuing down the Mt. Judah spur trail takes you past rounded Donner Peak (and usually a host of rock climbers) and side trails, which take you to excellent views of Donner Pass.

Directions: Take I-80 to the Soda Springs exit and turn right on Donner Pass Road (historic Route 44) to Donner Pass, just beyond the Sugar Bowl ski area. Park at the pass, off the road on the right.

Donner Pass North   2   M   *Pacific Crest Trail, granite ridge, views*

This is a short but spectacular jaunt that gives one a hearty taste of High Sierra splendor. The trailhead is directly across the road; most of the vehicles in the parking area are there for points south, primarily Donner Peak and Mt. Judah. Heading one mile north on the PCT won't take you to the top of a mountain, but will bring you to the top of an open-granite ridge.

The trail rises to a shelf above the road; because the road imme-diately drops from Donner Pass, the views promptly begin. Donner Lake is visible below, with Truckee and Mt. Rose beyond. The gran-ite shelf widens as it passes appropriately named School Rock, where rock-climbing novices scale the granite cliffs above and below.

Beyond a small patch of forest, the trail switchbacks up a shade-less chaparral-covered slope to the crest of the spur ridge. Here, take off from the trail and wander easily across an open expanse of gran-ite. To the west rises Boreal Ridge, at its base Lake Angela. Looking north, Castle Peak looms above constantly buzzing I-80. The PCT continues from the ridge you just crested and drops across a forested basin, passing small, visible lakes on its way to the trailhead near the interstate rest area. Being only 3.5 miles between the trailheads, this stretch of the PCT is popular with runners and anyone craving the High Sierra experience with easy access.

Directions: Take I-80 to the Soda-Springs exit and turn right on Donner Pass Road (historic Route 44) to Donner Pass, just beyond the Sugar-Bowl ski area. Park at the pass, off the road on the right.

Summit Lake (7,380')   4   M   *Pacific Crest Trail, cedar-fir forest, lake*

From the trailhead, follow the trail signs to the Pacific Crest Trail. At the PCT, turn right (north) on the trail, crossing in a tunnel under I-80. North of the interstate, turn right on the Summit Lake Trail. Summit Lake is pretty, and it is a pleasant ramble through High Sierra Forest to get there, making it an excellent destination with children. However, I-80 traffic is never quite out of earshot.

Directions: Take the Boreal-Ski-Resort exit from I-80 just before Donner Summit. Follow signs along the frontage road to the Pacific-Crest-Trail parking. Do not park at the rest area.

Frog Cliff (8,653') 5 M/SC *Alpine forest, views of Castle Peak, Pacific Crest and Mt. Rose*

Same directions as Summit Lake, except that before reaching Summit Lake, turn uphill on the Warren Lake Trail to a saddle on the Castle Peak ridge. There is an awesome view of the Sierra Crest. From the saddle, venture east up a short, use–path to look down on the Frog-Cliff escarpment and Frog Lake far below. Do not attempt to descend to the lake. Warren Lake requires an overnight backpack, so day hikers must return to the trailhead from here.

Directions: See Summit Lake.

Grouse Ridge Area—A number of remarkable hikes can be accessed from Bowman Lake Road; most are interconnected in a network of trails through one of the most scenic regions in the North Sierra. The Grouse Ridge Roadless Area is the closest to a wilderness area between Granite Chief and Bucks Lake wildernesses.

Sierra Discovery Trail (4,560') 1 E *Interpretive signs, forest, meadow, Bear River Falls, dogs on leash*

This is an excellent and beautiful loop for anyone with little time, or is disabled, or just wants to take it casual on a pleasantly scenic walk. This is actually a PG&E recreational trail, so the many interpretive signs are not only a fine guide to the natural surroundings, but also explain the PG&E presence in these parts. From the trail-head at the restrooms, the paved path heads to a shelter where there is information for the curious. The trail continues on through a small stand of trees and then across a meadow on a wooden boardwalk.

During the late mountain spring, corn lilies rise on spiky stalks on both sides of the boardwalk. Beyond this, the trail enters the forest and soon reaches a wide footbridge over the Bear River. Across the small river, the loop begins. It is gravel, but well graded and suitable for wheelchairs. It is preferable to head right because the reverse route would entail some climbing at the end. Heading right, the trail makes a gradual descent through a pine-fir forest, with frequent stops to identify wildlife.

About halfway in the loop, where the trail levels out and skirts a broad meadow, look for a long, fallen tree extending out across the meadow. That fallen tree will support you and allow access to an exceptional profusion of tiger lilies, startlingly orange at close range. Back on the loop, the trail reaches Bear River and curves for a stroll along or near the river. With a barely noticeable ascent, the trail offers fine view and access to the shaded river. Appropriately, your final stop in the loop is Bear River Falls, easily visible from an observation deck. With a drop of ten feet, the falls are not spectacular, but still provide a nice respite from one's cares for a moment.

After the falls, the loop rounds a bend, and you're back at the footbridge and at the end of the loop. At the trailhead, there is a very scenic picnic area, with shaded tables and gentle river access on large rocks.

Directions: Take Bowman Lake Road (FR 18) from Highway 20 (four miles west of I-80), 0.6 miles to the signed small parking area on the left. There are restrooms and water at the trailhead.

Spaulding Lake via Pioneer Trail (5,900')   4   M   *South Yuba River, fir-oak forest, lake, Pioneer Trail*

This section of the Pioneer Trail begins on the north side of the South Yuba River. Look for a post in the trail just east of the small parking area. The trail, shaded by oaks, pines, and cedars, heads east. The river, though unseen, is not out of earshot.

In 0.25 miles, you arrive at a shaded clearing with a river view. In spring snowmelt, the river is thunderous through here; in late summer, it is a low-key semblance of its raging self. Look over at the base of the slope for a metal stake indicating the Pioneer Trail. A narrow, single-wide path angles here in rocky switchbacks up to a level contour across the open slope, with nice views of river.

Soon the trail switchbacks down, nearer the river and again into shade. Be aware of the small patches of poison oak along the trail. At a broad meadow, there are expansive views of the towering cliffs on the south side of the river canyon, a rugged escarpment with tall trees hugging its crags. After crossing a small creek trickling across the trail from a miniature dripping waterfall, the trail begins to climb, in switchbacks and contours, steadily upward. When the switchbacks end, the trail levels off through shaded forest.

When you reach the large pipe that transports water from Fuller to Spaulding lakes, cross the dry creek bed under the pipe. Take the trail beyond the pipe to the right, cross the wooden footbridge, and scramble down open granite to the lakeshore. From here, Red Top and Old Man mountains, Fordyce Canyon and Grouse Ridge are grandly visible. Be cautious with the empty creek channel near you. Pretty with rocks and pools when empty or a trickle, it becomes a deadly roaring torrent when water is channeled through here at various times during the day. Retrace your steps to the trailhead, or if a shuttle is arranged, follow the pipeline up to Fuller Lake.

Directions: Take Bowman Lake Road (FR 18) from Highway 20 (four miles west of I-80), one mile to the bridge across South Yuba River. A small amount of parking is available on the north side of the bridge.

Zion Hill (6,201')　3　M　*Cedar-fir forest, Blue Lake, superb views*

The view from the top of this Grouse-Ridge spur is jaw-dropping, and it is had with minimal effort. At the start, you are immediately faced with a fork. The left heads climbs, and the right stays level. Your easier and better option is to start heading uphill on the left. (The right fork is more direct to Zion Hill, but is also much steeper for a longer distance—when you return that way, you'll be glad that you aren't heading in the reverse direction.)

You ascend on the left-hand road, too rugged for anything but high-clearance, four-by-four vehicles, through a forest of cedar, fir, and ponderosa pine. About a half mile up, beyond a locked forest-service gate, the road levels into an even grade, climbing more gradually. After a couple of steep pitches, the road levels off to contour the slope. Soon Blue Lake comes into view, with Zion Hill rising south of it.

The road swings around to the east side of the lake and terminates at a small, private cabin. A use-path continues south, up and across granite outcrops along Blue Lake's east shore. From these outcrops, the Fordyce-Creek watershed opens up, a panorama consisting of Black Butte, Old Man Mountain (the peak resembling Half Dome), and Red Mountain with its radio towers. In season, the slopes below you are dense with fire-red Indian paintbrush. Continue to the south shore of the lake, along the outcrops or the lakeshore.

A path follows the south shore to the dam. From the south end of the dam, it is easy to find the used path that follows the gradually rising crest to the top. The path is a clear, single track, impossible to miss, and a relatively easy ascent along the ridgeline. The view from the top is expansive in every direction. Rucker and Fuller lakes lie to the west. Grouse Ridge looms to the north above Blue Lake. The Fordyce Creek watershed opens up in its High Sierra granite glory. Spaulding lies below to the southeast, and the thin strip of I-80 threads its way toward Yuba Gap. Far to the west, beyond the South Fork's deep gash of a canyon, the Sutter Buttes rise from the great flat valley.

Retrace your steps to the dam. Use caution around the dam—it is a high elevation for rattlesnakes, but timber rattlers, larger, faster, and more aggressive than the foothill variety, have been encountered here. To return to your vehicle, take the road below the dam, cross Rucker Creek flowing from Blue Lake, and keep heading down. It's a steep drop, and you'll be surprised by how quickly you are returned to the loop's end.

Directions: Take Bowman Lake Road (FR 18) from Highway 20 (four miles west of I-80), five miles to Forest Road 18.06, signed for Camp Liahona. Turn right and travel for 1.3 miles on an unpaved road, sometimes very rocky. High clearance is not necessary, but passenger vehicles must negotiate the road carefully in spots. When you reach an obvious clearing, park and walk a few yards farther on the road until you come to a fork in the road. This begins the loop.

Island Lake (6,875') 2 M *Red fir forest, scenic lakes, granite expanses*

A crown jewel of the North Sierra, this extremely scenic lake is set against dramatic granite cliffs. The one-mile walk from the trailhead past Feeley Lake at the base of red-hued Fall Creek Mountain and a handful of small lakes has been dubbed by some as the "Miracle Mile" for being a pleasant walk step-by-step. From Island Lake, trails branch out to blue-hued Penner Lake, and Round and Milk Lakes at the base of Grouse Ridge. On the west side of Island Lake, there is a moderately easy route along the spine of Fall Creek Mountain to its summit, affording a panoramic vista that includes the Lindsey and Culbertson lakes.

Directions: Take Bowman Lake Road (FR 18) from Highway 20 (four miles west of I-80) to the Carr Lake/Feeley Lake turnoff (FR 17). Take the unpaved road four miles to the trailhead at Carr Lake. This road has some very rocky stretches and is perhaps the worst access road in this guide, but low-clearance vehicles should have no problem.

Penner Lake (6,900') 5 M *Scenic lakes, pink granite expanses, views*

Penner Lake might be the bluest lake in the North Sierra and is definitely one of the most spectacularly scenic. Follow the directions to Island Lake. From the trailhead at Carr Lake, the trail to Penner Lake is the first trail junction encountered just before arriving at Island Lake. Penner Lake is a mostly pleasant 1.5 miles, along the western shore of Island Lake and then past the Crooked Lakes. These small lakes are visible from a distance, glimpsed through trees, and offer little, if any, access.

There is a 0.25-mile climb up switchbacks, and then Penner Lake stretches before you, its sapphire blueness highlighted by the surrounding basin of pink granite. The trail is routed along the lake's eastern shore, where a few great camping/picnic spots are tucked into the firs and rock outcrops. This is one place where you don't need to feel limited to the trail. Penner Lake invites rambling around its scenic edges. Use care on the ridge that forms a massive western wall encasing the lake—it's a long drop to Culbertson Lake beyond and far below.

If you follow the trail to the crest of the hill at the north end of the lake, there is a short, easy scramble to the unnamed summit, from which not only is Penner Lake stretched out below, but the view in all directions is amazing. As with the vistas from Grouse Ridge and Fall Creek Mountain, the panorama is one of the most exceptional in the Grouse Ridge area.

Directions: Take Bowman Lake Road (FR 18) from Highway 20 (four miles west of I-80) to the Carr Lake/Feeley Lake turnoff (FR 17). Take the unpaved road four miles to the trailhead at Carr Lake. This road has some very rocky stretches and is perhaps the worst access road in this guide, but low-clearance vehicles should have no problem.

Grouse Ridge (7500')   1-3   M   *Views*

The road to Grouse Ridge is always one of the last roads in the North Sierra to be free of snow because it is one of the highest in elevation. It's also one of the few places where you can drive to the *top* of a ridge in the Sierra. Besides offering the best trail access to the Grouse Lakes Basin, for nonhikers and the physically challenged, it is also an ideal destination for sharing the glory that is the breathtaking vista of the High Sierra. You don't even need to leave your vehicle at the trailhead parking to take in the panorama.

It's there, virtually spread out before you. You'd be cheating yourself, though, if you didn't get out to smell the rarefied air and listen to the rustle of a breeze through the firs or the trill of a high-altitude bird. You can stretch your legs along the ridgetop without walking the half mile down into the forest and granite basin below, to Milk Lake directly below and the network of trails to a variety of beautiful destinations. Short trails on the ridge provide access to the summits.

From the trailhead parking, follow the road that continues uphill to the former lookout. A locked gate blocks vehicular access at about 0.25 miles. Another quarter mile, and the road levels off on the peak. The view from the old lookout, being restored as a guest facility, is as exceptional as you would expect from a fire lookout. After enjoying the vista and returning to the parking area, you can then go exploring on a trail that extends through the forest service campground, merge with the Grouse Ridge Trail briefly before heading to the left and up to the eastern summit. It is a great option to spend a casual day on Grouse Ridge.

Directions: Take Bowman Lake Road (FR 18) from Highway 20 (four miles west of I-80), about six miles to Grouse Ridge Road, and turn right. The unpaved forest road climbs steadily but gradually for six miles, with a couple of steep pitches. It should be no problem for passenger vehicles. Drive past the campground to the parking area for hikers. Do not continue upward to the summit because the road is blocked by a locked metal gate about 0.25 miles up.

Downey Lake (7400')   2   S   *Scenic Sierra lake in granite basin*

For a short jaunt from Grouse Ridge down to one of the nearby lakes, this is your most scenic option. It is the same distance from the trailhead to Downey Lake as Milk Lake nestled just below Grouse Ridge, but with only a fraction of visitors due to Milk Lake's much-easier access. At just short of 0.5 miles down the Grouse Ridge Trail, the Downey Lake Trail cuts off on the right.

In 0.3 miles the trail drops steeply down a rocky draw to a superior camping spot on the western shore of Downey Lake. The entire like is granite-ringed more than most in this area. Sand Ridge looms across the northern horizon. An informal path heads south to a small dam and past it to a narrow gap with a view down Fordyce Creek Canyon. I-80 is visible along a distant ridge in a thin ribbon of asphalt. What makes Downey Lake special isn't just the superlative Sierra landscape, but also the strong sense of solitude. Downey Lake sees a fraction of the "hordes" at Island Lake, and that fraction might be only you.

Directions: Take Bowman Lake Road (FR 18) from Highway 20 (four miles west of I-80), about six miles to Grouse Ridge Road, and turn right. The unpaved forest road climbs steadily but gradually for six miles, with a couple of steep pitches. It should be no problem for passenger vehicles. Drive past the campground to the parking area for hikers. Do not continue upward to the summit because the road is blocked by a locked metal gate about 0.25 miles up.

Glacier Lake (7,550') 9.2 M/SL *Views, Sand Ridge, scenic lakes, wildflowers*

Glacier Lake, at the eastern edge of the Grouse Lakes Roadless Area, is a nice-enough lake, but the real reason for doing this hike is the journey itself. The hike can be done from the Carr Lake Trailhead; it's a very pretty route, but it also adds three miles to the round-trip mileage. The best option for a day hike is the Grouse-Ridge trailhead. There the view is already breathtaking before you even take one step. The Grouse Lakes Basin lies before you, with Milk Lake directly below. The Sierra Buttes crown the horizon to the north, with English Mountain to its right, and to the right of that is long Sand Ridge stretching to Black Butte. The Sand Ridge Trail is visible, where it snakes up the western end of the ridge.

Setting out on the trail from the lower end of the parking area, you drop easterly down the ridge crest in a gentle descent. The views are constant. Sanford Lake becomes visible below to the east. (The access trail to that lake is from the campground.) At about 0.5 miles, just before reaching the basin floor, you'll pass the trail down to Downey Lake. 0.10 miles beyond this is the junction with the Round Lake Trail coming in on the left. Milk Lake is "just around the bend," so close the trail sign doesn't give a mileage.

Continuing north on the Grouse Ridge Trail, you soon arrive at the junction with the Glacier Lake Trail on the right. Take it and cross a wet meadow to another trail junction. A sign indicates that the lower trail is to Glacier Lake. This path is routed through forest and meadows, usually occupied by grazing cattle in summer, and is slightly more direct to Glacier Lake, but the upper unmarked trail will also get you to Glacier Lake with maximum scenery. This trail is the one you want. The trail is the rocky remnant of an old mining road and climbs gradually at first.

Halfway up the ridge, the trail ascends through a broad meadow, gorgeous with yellow mule's ears. Only as you approach the top does the trail climb more seriously, and views emerge of Grouse Ridge and Downey Lake tucked in its nearly treeless granite bowl. The incongruous ding of a cowbell may drift up from somewhere below. As you crest Sand Ridge at almost 7,400 feet, the view is stupendous in all directions. The entire Grouse Lakes Basin is displayed from Grouse Ridge north to Red Hill, with brick-red Fall Creek Mountain in between directly to the west. Farther north the Sierra Buttes ruggedly make their jagged claim on the horizon. To the northeast stand Haystack and English mountains. Black Butte ridge are the dark ramparts across the eastern horizon. Glacier Lake sits at the base of that dark ridge, up past the highest little forest grove.

The route along Sand Ridge is a classic amble. This is a stroll with tremendous mountain views and meadows riotous with wildflowers. At the eastern edge of the ridge, the trail drops, but not too far. Where it becomes indistinct, follow it to the left, down a rocky wash. Rock cairns along the way keep you on the correct route. Shortly you reach a broad granite expanse, a near-white shelf peppered with twisted firs. From the rim of this shelf, you peer down into the Five Lakes Basin, and from here, you can see all five tiny lakes.

Returning to your trail, it becomes a narrow one-track. After passing a string of pretty granite-bound ponds, the trail climbs through the final forested approach to Glacier Lake. There can be snow still on the ground in midsummer, and if the trail disappears, keep heading up in an obvious direction and the trail reemerges. Glacier Lake, at 7,240 feet, fills a rocky bowl at the base of craggy Black Butte, towering only a few hundred feet above the lake. There are several fine campsites, some with a view west to the Sierra Buttes, which makes for memorable sunsets. A semi loop can be made by returning on the Glacier Lake Trail, which leaves the lake at its southwest corner.

Directions: Take Bowman Lake Road (FR 18) from Highway 20 (four miles west of I-80), about six miles to Grouse Ridge Road, and turn right. The unpaved forest road climbs steadily but gradually for six miles, with a couple of steep pitches. It should be no problem for passenger vehicles. Drive past the campground to the parking area for hikers. Do not continue upward to the summit because the road is blocked by a locked metal gate about 0.25 miles up.

Loney Meadow (6,000')   1.5   E   *Sierra meadow, Texas Creek*

You're not likely to encounter many others on this quiet, easy loop. Few know of its existence, or where it is. Here you can experience the Sierra from a meadow's perspective, with solitude and silence. The loop trail circumnavigates through forest fringe on the south, eastern, and northern edges of the broad, flat meadow. At the eastern end of the meadow, just past the footbridge over gurgling Texas Creek, a signed trail heads east to Culbertson Lake (and a possible loop including the Lindsey Lakes) and to the Grouse-Ridge trail network.

The route along the western portion of the meadow involves a wooden boardwalk and is impassable during snowmelt, when Texas Creek inundates the meadow. The other trails are very accessible at that time, but it's temporarily not a loop. The view from the west edge of the meadow is possibly the most scenic spot on the trail, with the meadow stretching toward Bowman Mountain and a prominent unnamed peak to the south and nearer.

Directions: Take Bowman Lake Road (FR 18) from Highway 20 (four miles west of I-80) beyond the Carr-Feeley turnoff to the end of the pavement. Bowman Lake Road continues, and the access road to Loney Meadows is just ahead on the right. If not driving farther, park here and walk the half mile to the trailhead. Otherwise, turn right and take every left fork when given a choice. The trailhead is clearly signed, with parking for many vehicles.

North Yuba River—Not only is Highway 49 along the North Yuba one of the prettiest riverside drives in the state, it provides access to several nice trails, which are usually open when the higher mountains are still covered with snow. In autumn, the roadside is a veritable celebration of the big-leaf maples' transition to brilliant yellow gold, particularly the twelve-mile stretch between Downieville and Sierra City.

Canyon Creek Trail (2,000') 3–6 E *Old mining road, North Yuba River*

This broad, flat, old road (Indian Valley Road on maps) provides a pleasant stroll with scenic views of the North Yuba. Turn around at the Cherokee Creek footbridge because the next two miles contour along the wooded canyon slopes with no river views.

Directions: Traveling north on Highway 49, accessible from Marysville Road or Nevada City, into Sierra County, trailhead parking is on the left just after crossing the highway bridge over the North Yuba River.

Fiddle Creek Ridge (4,140') 3–7 M *Pine-oak forest, views of North Yuba Canyon and Sierra Buttes*

The shady trail first climbs up past an old ditch and then switchbacks up as the ridge crest rises. For three miles you ascend under a dense forest canopy. This is followed by about a mile of open vistas along the narrow ridge, with the North Yuba far below on the right and the Fiddle Creek drainage closer at hand on the left. If a shuttle is arranged, you can traverse the full seven miles by connecting with and descending to Highway 49 on the Halls Ranch Trail.

Directions: From Highway 49, just east of Indian Valley Store, take Cal-Ida Road, 0.25 miles to signed trailhead for Fiddle Creek Ridge. There is a small amount of parking across the road.

North Yuba Trail (2,200') 0.25–7 E *North Yuba River, forest*

From the Rocky Rest trailhead, a footbridge crosses the river. The trail then turns left for a pleasant riverside walk on the shady south bank for seven miles to the Gold Rush village of Goodyears Bar. The trail can be started from either end.

Directions: Same as Canyon Creek; travel a few miles farther to Rocky Rest Campground on Highway 49 at the eastern end of Indian Valley Recreation Area. Trailhead is inside campground, next to river.

Halls Ranch Trail (4,140')   3–7   M   *Fiddle Creek Ridge*

This old ranch access trail provides access to the eastern end of Fiddle Creek Ridge Trail. From the parking area, cross the highway. The signed trail takes off from the access road to the Ramshorn summer home tract (not the Ramshorn Campground just up Highway 49). You switchback up through a shady forest of Douglas fir, black oak, and canyon live oak. "Up" is the key word here, as you ascend about 1,500 feet.

In places, the rail snakes across open, south-facing slopes. Your views from these open areas are primarily of the steep wooded slopes of Pliocene Ridge across the canyon. The roar of the rushing North Yuba and the occasional hum from vehicles drift up from the canyon bottom. As you climb, these sounds fade, leaving only the whoosh of wind through the trees. It's about 1.5 miles from trailhead to the crest of Fiddle Creek Ridge.

Follow the trail west along the crest about 0.25 miles to a high point with views in all directions. The Sierra Buttes loom fortress-like fifteen miles to the east, at the top of the densely forested North Yuba River canyon. Closer, about two miles away at Goodyears Bar, sits the rocky face of Grizzly Peak. For those not continuing on west along to the Fiddle Creek end of the trail (it is seven miles from trailhead to trailhead), this is a good place to turn around.

Directions: Signed trailhead parking is on Highway 49 at Indian Rock Picnic Area, two miles west of Goodyears Bar.

Haypress-Wild Plum Loop (4,840')   3.5   M   *Fir forest, creeks, view of Sierra Buttes*

Usually free of snow earlier than trails higher up, this pleasant loop on part of the Pacific Crest Trail features unique from-the-east views of the Sierra Buttes and an unseen but audible waterfall. Except for the first half mile, the loop is either level or downhill. On foot from the parking area, cross the auto bridge into the campground. Go to Sites 20-47, where the road is blocked by an iron gate. Continue past the gate for a long half mile of an uphill jeep road. There is little shade, and the natural experience is tempered by the presence of power lines parallel to the road. At the top, there is another metal gate and a wooden bridge over Hilda Mine Creek.

There is another one hundred unshaded feet farther to the signed Haypress Creek Trail on the left. The strenuous part of the hike is over. Leave the road and head off on the trail shaded by firs and cedars. The trail exits the trees and crosses open slopes covered with scrubby manzanita. Where the trail veers to a sharp right, look left for the first of stunning views of the Sierra Buttes' eastern flanks.

From this vantage, the sawtooth configuration of the buttes is hidden, and the mountain looks almost volcanically conical. Gradually descend to a junction with the PCT and a footbridge over Haypress Creek. There is a pretty cascade just upstream, visible from the bridge. Across the bridge, the trail begins to wend its way down the canyon. Soon the roar of Haypress Falls rumbles on your left. Tucked deep in an inner gorge of Haypress Creek, the falls are inaccessible and unseen. There is no known vantage point from which to see the falls, and it is not advisable to attempt scrambling down into the gorge.

Farther along the trail, a rock outcrop provides an awesome view of the buttes and the North Yuba River canyon. Beyond this, watch for the junction with the Wild Plum Trail on the left. Leave the PCT and descend on shaded switchbacks. The trail levels out, and Haypress Creek bubbles alongside unseen. After passing some abandoned forest-service buildings, the loop's end is reached at the campground bridge.

Directions: From Highway 49 in the north end of Sierra City, turn right on the road signed for Wild Plum Campground and follow it for about two miles to the campground and park in the area designated for day hikers. Do not proceed into the campground unless you are occupying a campsite.

Loves Falls (4,800')   1   E   *Waterfall on North Yuba River*

From Highway 49, take the Pacific Crest Trail for a half mile on a barely discernible descent to the footbridge across North Yuba River. The waterfall is directly below the bridge. About thirty feet before the bridge, a side trail provides steep access to the river and excellent views of the falls. It is exceptionally impressive in spring when snowmelt is raging down the river.

Directions: The Pacific Crest Trail crosses Highway 49 about a mile north of Sierra City. There are pullouts for parking.

Sierra Buttes / Lakes Basin—This region is like a secret national park, with a wide variety of hikes for every taste. All but the last trail are accessed from Gold Lake Highway.

Haskell Peak (8,107')   4   M   *Alpine forest, views of Sierra Buttes and Sierra Valley*

This is a relatively easy two-mile walk to the second highest peak in the Sierra Buttes region. The trail begins across the road and, for the most part, is a moderate ramble through a small meadow and mixed-fir forest. The trail is steep in one brief section, constructed in the Swiss alpine manner: straight up without switchbacks. From the peak, there are excellent views to the west of the Sierra crest from the Sierra Buttes north to Mt. Elwell; and to the east of the broad Sierra Valley, the largest valley in the entire Sierra range, similar to the parks of the Colorado Rockies. The array of wildflowers along the trail in midsummer is amazing.

Directions: Take Highway 49, five miles past Sierra City to the old stage stop of Bassetts, and turn left on Gold Lake Highway. Take Gold Lake Highway past Sardine Lake Road to Haskell Peak

Road (Forest Road 09) on the right. Turn onto the unpaved but well-graded road for nine miles to trailhead parking on the right.

Sand Pond Loop (5,762')   1   E   *Interpretive signs*

A flat path through pleasant woods with a plank walkway over a beaver pond and postcard views of the Sierra Buttes. Great for kids and nonhikers. Glacial and mining history are highlighted with the natural history. Flying squirrels are native to this area.

Directions: Take Highway 49, five miles past Sierra City to the old stage stop of Bassetts, and turn left on Gold Lake Highway. Take Gold Lake Highway to Sardine Lake Road, turn left, and proceed across Salmon Creek, past Packer Lake Road. Parking is on the left, just past the campground.

Upper Sardine Lake (5,900')   2   M   *Scenic lake at base of Sierra Buttes*

From the end of the paved road, follow the rugged old mining road that hugs the mountain slope above Lower Sardine Lake. Occasionally, there might be a high-clearance vehicle to step aside for, but the old road is prohibitive for most vehicles. At the top of the lower lake, traces of the Young American Mine are visible. Upper Sardine Lake, only a mile from the trailhead, sits spectacularly at the base of the towering Sierra Buttes. There are many spots along the rocky shoreline from which to enjoy the view.

Directions: Take Highway 49, five miles past Sierra City to the old stage stop of Bassetts, and turn left on Gold Lake Highway. Take Gold Lake Highway to Sardine Lake Road, turn left, and proceed across Salmon Creek, past Packer Lake Road and Sand Pond to the end of the paved road at Sardine Lake Lodge.

Tamarack Trail (7,070') 5.7 M *Views of Sardine Lakes and Sierra Buttes*

The trail is an old mining road, very rocky in the exposed sections. As the trail rises gradually along the glacial moraine, expansive views grow of both Sardine Lakes and, breathtakingly, the Sierra Buttes. At the forested top of the ridge, you can rest in the shade and enjoy the panorama. The trail continues on to the Tamarack Lakes, but this is a good place to turn around and return to the trailhead—it is downhill all the way.

Directions: Take Highway 49, five miles past Sierra City to the old stage stop of Bassetts, and turn left on Gold Lake Highway. Take Gold Lake Highway to Sardine Lake Road, turn left, and proceed across Salmon Creek. Trailhead is on the right just past Packer Lake Road and before the campground.

Mountain Mine Trail (7,020') 6 M *Best view of Sierra Buttes*

The trail is another old mining road. It passes the edge of the campground, then fords Sardine Creek, and rounds the end of the glacial moraine. Here it climbs gradually, hugging the mountainside, with expanding views of the North Yuba canyon. (About halfway, a trail cuts up to the right to Volcano Lake, but this is on private land.) At two miles, the trail rounds a point; and for the final mile, you have a stunningly close-up view of the upper Sierra Buttes across a canyon. At trail's end is the site of Mountain Mine. If you climb up on the saddle above the mine, Upper Sardine Lake is visible. Return the way you came.

Directions: Take Highway 49, five miles past Sierra City to the old stage stop of Bassetts, and turn left on Gold Lake Highway. Take Gold Lake Highway to Sardine Lake Road, turn left, and proceed across Salmon Creek. Trailhead is across from Packer Lake Road, where there is space for parking.

Sierra Buttes (8,591')   5.2–7   SC   *Views, western white pine/lodge-pole/hemlock forest*

The centerpieces of most national parks (e.g. Yosemite Valley, Grand Canyon, and Old Faithful in Yellowstone) all exert a pull that draws people to do nothing more than just be there. The craggy Sierra Buttes have that same kind of pull. Visible from the Sacramento Valley, they loom above the surrounding mountains like a bit of the Rockies resting on the Sierra. From far away or nearby, the buttes resemble a fortress stronghold of old, a rocky sentinel dominating the landscape.

There are a multitude of trails to the summit, ranging in length from 4 miles to the grueling 8.5 miles on the shadeless Pacific Crest Trail from Highway 49 near Sierra City. The shortest, most direct route is from Packer Lake Saddle on a mix of single-track and jeep trails. Along the way, it is easy to go over to rim and look out on the eagle's-eye view of the glacial cirque gouged out of the ridge. The two Sardine lakes in a row, and just below, inaccessible from any direction, Young America Lake, the highest body of water in the Sardine Creek drainage. The final approach to the lookout perched on a rugged pinnacle is a metal stairway extending along an open rock face. Anyone with heights issues is advised to go no further and be satisfied that the view is pretty good from where they are.

Directions: Take Highway 49, five miles past Sierra City to the old stage stop of Bassetts, and turn left on Gold Lake Highway. Take Gold Lake Highway to Sardine Lake Road, turn left, and proceed across Salmon Creek. At Packer Lake Road, turn right and drive a little over four miles to Packer Lake Saddle. The road is paved the entire distance, but the final mile to the top of the ridge is steep and narrow. The trailhead, with ample parking, is 0.5 miles south along the ridge.

Deer Lake (7,090')   5   M   *Scenic lake, aspen groves, view of Sierra Buttes*

The trail begins across the road. This is a highly scenic walk that climbs gradually through High Sierra scenery, including aspen groves, which are a brilliant golden in autumn. At a junction with the trail to Salmon Lake, head west to Deer Lake. This is one of the prettiest lakes in the region, with panoramic views of the Sierra Buttes. The Pacific Crest Trail runs along the ridge above the lake and provides even more expansive vistas.

Directions: Take Highway 49, five miles past Sierra City to the old stage stop of Bassetts, and turn left on Gold Lake Highway. Take Gold Lake Highway to Sardine Lake Road, turn left, and proceed across Salmon Creek. Turn right on Packer Lake Road and continue for 2.7 miles to trailhead parking on the left at Packsaddle Campground.

Lower Salmon Lake (6,550')　2　E　*Forest, quiet lake, old mine*

This serene lake is perfect for anyone who wants a short, easy walk away from the hum and bustle of civilization. It makes a great backpack site for introducing kids to the great outdoors. From Salmon Lake Road, walk down the old jeep road. It is an easy ramble as the road disappears, and sooner than you expect, you're at the north shore of the destination lake. It is nothing remarkable, no scenic backdrop or rocky shoreline. Just a small quiet lake hemmed in by reeds and dense forest down to the water on most sides.

A few nice picnic or campsites can be found to the right along the lake, but judging from the boggy fringes around the lake, I'd have plenty of mosquito repellent on hand. An old jeep trail circles around the western edge of the lake to a well-preserved, old mine, complete with old, narrow-gauge rail tracks emerging from the boarded-up entrance. In the area southwest of the lake, look for traces of an old, burned-out miner's shack. When done savoring the peacefulness here, it's an easy saunter back to the road.

Directions: Take Highway 49, five miles past Sierra City to the old stage stop of Bassetts, and turn left on Gold Lake Highway. Take Gold Lake Highway to Salmon Lake Road on the left. Take that road 0.5 miles to the trailhead for Lower Salmon Lake.

Frazier Falls (6,180')   1   E   *Impressive waterfall, handicapped-access, good for kids, dogs on leash*

The trail is short, paved, and usually packed with people, but the falls, 176 feet high, are worth it, especially after snowmelt. Morning provides the best light for viewing the falls.

Directions: Take Highway 49, five miles past Sierra City to the old stage stop of Bassetts, and turn left on Gold Lake Highway. Take Gold Lake Highway to Frazier Falls Road on the right at the junction with the Gold Lake turnoff. Turn right onto the unpaved but well-graded road for 4.2 miles to paved trailhead parking.

Round Lake Loop (7,020')   4.5   M   *Scenic lakes, views of Mt Elwell and Lakes Basin, old mine*

This is a High Sierra hike without the backpacks. From the trailhead, take the Round Lake Trail, initially passing the rustic cabins of Gold Lake Lodge. At a fork, either direction works for the loop. Taking the righthand path, you drop into a meadow then pass the three charming Bear Lakes. The loop, gradually climbing, passes scenic Long, Silver, and Round lakes before arriving at the site of an old mine above Round Lake, with an exceptional view of the Lakes Basin. Continue on the loop for a gradual descent to the trailhead.

Directions: Take Highway 49, five miles past Sierra City to the old stage stop of Bassetts, and turn left on Gold Lake Highway. Take Gold Lake Highway to signed trailhead parking for Round Lake, about a mile past Frazier Falls Road.

Mt. Elwell (7,818')   7   M/SC   *Scenic lakes, views of Lakes Basin and Sierra Buttes*

From the trailhead, follow signs to Long and Silver Lakes, and from Silver Lake to Mt. Elwell. This is a nice hike through varying scenery, much with a wilderness effect. The final ascent of the peak is an uphill climb, but the views are worth it, especially the panoramic High Sierra ridge south to the Sierra Buttes.

Directions: Take Highway 49, five miles past Sierra City to the old stage stop of Bassetts, and turn left on Gold Lake Highway. Take Gold Lake Highway to sign for Mt. Elwell Lodge. Turn left and follow road to trailhead parking.

Fern Falls (6,160')   1   M   *Waterfall, view of Graeagle Creek Canyon, good for kids*

This short loop offers dramatic scenery, a sweet little waterfall, and a well-placed picnic table for savoring the delightful vista of Gray Eagle Creek's tumbling course from Mt. Elwell. Kids and nonhikers will enjoy it because the walking is minimal and whimsical in the manner of a child's fantasy forest path. The trail is an obvious path from the pullout down to a footbridge across East Gray Eagle Creek and then one hundred yards to a Y in the trail.

Those who would prefer heading for the nearby table can take the left fork and soon be up on the flat spot, where a grand panorama can be enjoyed while sitting. Those who want to see the falls and complete the short loop will take the right fork. That leg of the loop swings down near the creek. You'll hear Fern Falls before dropping to a view of the pretty waterfall. The loop then continues around a pronounced promontory to the picnic table. From this point, Mt. Elwell towers impressively to the southwest.

Directions: Though unsigned, the trailhead here is at a wide pullout on the west side of Gold Lake Highway, 1.1 miles up from the Gray Eagle Lodge turnoff.

Jamison/Rock Lakes (6,300')   7.5   M   *Scenic lakes, view of Mt. Elwell*

The pleasant trail follows Jamison Creek to very scenic Jamison and Rock lakes, picturesquely located beneath the east slopes of Mt. Elwell. Add a mile if you make a side trip to nearby Wade Lake.

Directions: Take Highway 49, five miles past Sierra City to the old stage stop of Bassetts, and turn left on Gold Lake Highway. Take Gold Lake Highway to Highway 89 and turn left, passing through the resort village of Graeagle to Plumas-Eureka State Park. In the park, turn left on the signed turnoff for Jamison Lake and follow the unpaved road to the trailhead at Jamison Mine.

Bucks Lake Wilderness—Northernmost Sierra ridge, adjacent to Bucks Lake, with panoramic vistas north to the Southern Cascades. One of the largest-known stands of old-growth red fir cover the south-facing slopes.

Spanish Peak (7,075')   7   M   *Scenic lakes, rim walk, views, red fir botanical preserve*

This is an outstanding hike with a great variety of scenery. Your route starts on the Gold Lake Trail, which crosses Silver Lake's shallow dam and spillway and, in a few steps, enters the wilderness. After climbing the side of a glacial moraine, the trail crosses the low crest and maintains a fairly even keel along the moraine to a trail junction. Take the Granite Gap Trail.

The climb begins immediately, the ascent often on well-crafted stairs of granite blocks. The trade-off for your effort is the constantly expanding view of the granite escarpment on either side. In no other part of the North Sierra is there a trail that climbs the wall more or less straight up a thousand-foot escarpment. The final 0.25-mile climbs up a wooded draw to the rim, and the panoramic view temporarily vanishes. At the top, turn left onto the Pacific Crest Trail, with an easy stroll along a Sierra rim through the fringe of an old-growth red-fir forest. Spanish Peak, well signed and easily reached—on an old utility road—still has the foundation of a long-gone fire lookout. The view is exceptional of the escarpment, Lake Almanor, and on the horizon, Lassen Peak. This is the northernmost Sierra ridge—you are looking north to the Cascades.

Directions: From Highway 70 in Oroville, take Highway 162, Oro Dam Boulevard, east into the hills. Wind past Lake Oroville—beyond the lake, Highway162 becomes Oroville–Quincy Highway. Beyond the community of Berry Creek, the paved road becomes winding, but on an even grade. Pass the community of Bucks Lake, and after a sharp descent (there is an alternate route on Big Creek Road, longer but more gradual), turn left on Silver Lake Road. Follow the unpaved road to the trailhead at Silver Lake.

Gold Lake (6,000')   3.1   E *Scenic lakes, Spanish Peak*

Scenic Gold Lake sits at the base of towering Spanish Peak. Follow the directions for Spanish Peak. At the trail junction with the Granite Gap Trail, continue on the left trail across the slopes to Gold Lake.

Directions: From Highway 70 in Oroville, take Highway 162, Oro Dam Boulevard, east into the hills. Wind past Lake Oroville—beyond the lake, Highway162 becomes Oroville–Quincy Highway. Beyond the community of Berry Creek, the paved road becomes winding, but on an even grade. Pass the community of Bucks Lake, and after a sharp descent (there is an alternate route on Big Creek Road, longer but more gradual), turn left on Silver Lake Road. Follow the unpaved road to the trailhead at Silver Lake.

North Sacramento Valley—*The flat-as-a-pancake valley rolls into shallow hills in Tehama County and then larger hills as it stretches through Redding to the Klamath Mountains. Redding is a walker's paradise, plus a vast network of trails is found in the River-Bend area near Red Bluff, and four waterfalls invite exploration in the Whiskeytown Lake area. Vegetation is predominately blue oak woodland, except for broad, grassy savannahs and the Payne Creek wetlands around Big Bend.*

Redding Area
McConnell Arboretum
Sacramento River Trail
Churn Creek Open Space
Clover Creek Preserve
Chamise Peak
Westside Trail
Mule Mountain Loop
Clear Creek Trail
Piety Hill Loop
Cloverdale Loop

Sacramento River Bend Outstanding Natural Area
Iron Canyon Loop
Hog Lake Plateau and Vista Trail
Paynes Creek Wetlands
Coyote Pond
Perry Riffle Trail
Osprey Pond
Massacre Flat

Whiskeytown Lake National Recreation Area
Brandy Creek Falls
Boulder Creek Falls
Whiskeytown Falls

Iron Canyon

Redding Area—A guide could be written just for the Redding area, with more than eighty-two miles of well-graded trails in and round the Redding basin. Tucked into the wooded northernmost portion of the Sacramento Valley, closely hemmed in by mountains on three sides, Redding is one of the prettiest cities in the state.

McConnell Arboretum (472') 1.5–2.7 E Sundial Bridge, Sacramento River, handicapped-access

Start by crossing the gracefully unique Sundial Bridge, Northern California's newest landmark, over the river. From the north end of the bridge, the arboretum is to the left, with its flat paths for ambling among examples of native and exotic vegetation. To the right of the bridge's north end is a 1.2-mile loop through an oak woodland, reclaimed from gravel quarries used during construction of Shasta Dam. Access points for the Sacramento River Trail are also located at both ends of the bridge.

Directions: From I-5, take Highway 44 west toward downtown Redding and exit at the first off-ramp signed for Sundial Bridge. Turn right from the exit and shortly reach the parking area on the right for Turtle Bay.

Sacramento River Trail (562') 6 E Sacramento River, where it emerges from mountains

Broad and flat, the paved trail allows for strolls on both sides of the river, with scenic views of the rising canyon slopes and much river access. The trail can be accessed from many points, including the end of Bechelli Lane at the trail's southern end and Court Street upstream, but the easiest access is at the Sundial Bridge.

Directions: From I-5, take Highway 44 west toward downtown Redding and exit at the first off-ramp signed for Sundial Bridge. Turn right from the exit and shortly reach the parking area on the right for Turtle Bay.

Churn Creek Open Space (495')   4   E   *Blue oak woodland, shallow hills*

Paved or gravel paths wander among shallow rolling hills through an oak woodland. Primarily used by locals, there are numerous access points from the surrounding neighborhood, all obscure. You can also enter the open space from adjacent Lema Ranch, but dogs are prohibited in that park and would hinder walking your dog from that direction. The easiest access is from Minder Park.

Directions: From I-5, take Highway 44 east to Victor Avenue (first exit). Take Victor Avenue north (left from exit) to Old Alturas Road. Turn right on Old Alturas Road, a short distance to Edgewood Drive, and turn left. Follow Edgewood a few blocks and turn right on Tiburon Drive. The next left is Minder Drive, which you take to its end at Minder Park. The trailhead for the open space is just beyond the small playground.

Clover Creek Preserve (485')   1–3   E   *Vernal pools*

Located in southeast Redding, this is a former flood-detention basin. It still provides flood control downstream, but is now primarily a vernal pool habitat with Clover Creek as a centerpiece. Mixed paved and gravel paths thread through the 123 acres of grassy meadows. A small blue oak woodland occupies the northeast corner of the preserve.

Directions: From I-5, take the Churn Creek / Bonnyview exit and head east on Churn Creek Road. Veer left uphill on Rancho Road. On Rancho Road, take the fifth left turn onto Shasta View Drive. On Shasta View, turn right at Venus Way for the entrance to the preserve.

Chamise Peak (1,601')   4.8   M   *Blue oak woodland, views*

This is an easy, very nice, two-mile ascent to a flat-topped peak with excellent views. From the trailhead on the Flanagan Trail, the single-track path winds gradually but steadily up through manzanita, valley oaks, and gray pines. In 1.2 miles, at a trail junction, take the right fork signed for Chamise Peak. Wind the final 0.8 miles to the shaved-off mountaintop, where a picnic table has been placed. Besides the view of Shasta dam and lake with Mt. Shasta rising beyond, the vista includes the river canyon below and, to the southeast, the silvery gleam of the Sacramento River through the Turtle-Bay section of Redding, with Lassen Peak on the horizon.

Directions: From I-5 north of Redding, take the Pine Grove exit and head west. At Lake Boulevard, turn right. In 0.8 miles, turn left on Flanagan Road and follow it 1.2 miles to its end at a locked gate. On the right is a small parking area and a sign for the Flanagan Trail.

Westside Trail (1,250')   2   M   *Ridgetop route, best views of Redding*

Located on a ridge in west Redding, this offers an aerial view of the Redding area. From your vehicle, walk up the paved continuation of Skywalker, which is, at this point, blocked off to vehicular traffic. From here, you look down steep slopes covered with gray pine, blue oak, and manzanita. At a saddle in the ridge crest, the unpaved trail to the vista point bears to the right.

The trail winds to the flat peak for a 360-degree panorama of the best view of Redding to be found without benefit of aircraft. East is the Redding basin and Lassen Peak beyond. Mt. Shasta rises to the north, with Castle Crags left of it on the horizon. That high peak to the west is Shasta Bally. It is about a half mile from the end of Skywalker Road to the vista point. You can continue to explore the ridge, or if a shuttle is arranged, head down to one of the lower trailheads on Valparaiso Road, Rattlesnake Road, or Mary Lake.

Directions: To reach the highest trailhead with the least amount of climbing, take Placer Street/Road from downtown Redding. Heading southwest, it becomes County Road A-16. Two miles past Buenaventura Boulevard, turn right on O'Conner. Turn left on Tralee to Dillon, and left on Dillon, to the top of the road at Skywalker. Turn right and park at the end of Skywalker.

Mule Mountain Loop (953') 8 M *Oak woodland, views of Whiskeytown Lake and Shasta Bolly*

Swasey Recreation Area is a BLM unit. Mostly a rolling landscape of blue oaks and gray pines, it offers a network of easy paths that ramble through the dense woodland. The one exception to the easy rambling is the loop up onto Mule Mountain to the west, where the BLM unit adjoins Whiskeytown NRA. From the Meiners Trailhead, head due east, past the yellow metal gate on an old road. After dipping to cross a seasonal creek, the route goes straight up the opposite slope about one-third mile to a sign for Mule Mountain. Beyond this, the trail levels out and narrows to a real single-track path.

At a junction with Mule Mountain Trail, take the right fork. The trail gradually climbs up a pleasant canyon beside a pretty seasonal brook and then up through ridgetop avenues of manzanita, offering brief fantasy-like passage. Where the slope steepens, switchbacks ease the ascent. Except for a few open patches, the trail is pleasantly shaded by maples and oaks. Poison oak shows up in dense clusters along the trail.

At Mule Mountain Pass is a picnic table and a junction of trails. The Mule Mountain Trail is with a left-or-right choice onto Mule Ridge, and the trail to Whiskeytown Lake NRA head downhill to the west. To the northeast, the Escalator Trail, your return route, descends. Any views from the pass are obscured by trees, so to see anything, scramble up a spur path northward along the ridge. A short, strenuous climb brings views of Mule Mountain to the south and Shasta Bally to the west. Whiskeytown Lake can be glimpsed through the trees, with the primordial skyline of the Trinity Alps beyond. Eastward, Lassen Peak dominates the horizon.

On your return route, the Escalator Trail meanders on a contour along the ridge. Shaded initially, the trail emerges into the open, with panoramic vistas of the Redding basin and down the Sacramento Valley. As befits its almost-level, contour status, the descent is very gradual, as would be the ascent in reverse. The trail continues to wind down a spur ridge like a snake laid out down the slope. At the junction with Meiners Loop, either direction will return you to the trailhead.

Directions: From downtown Redding, take Placer Street/Road, also known as County Road A-16. Four miles from Buenaventura Boulevard, turn right onto Swasey Road. It is 1.1 mile on Swasey Road to the signed entrance to Swasey Recreation Area on the left. It is a mile into the recreation area on a well-graded gravel road to its end at the Meiners Trailhead.

Clear Creek Trail (622')   1–5   E   *Creek-side route, small gorge with spawning salmon*

Four trailheads provide access to a flat creek-side trail through a riparian woodland. At a small gorge, an overlook offers salmon viewing, best from October 1 to December 1.

Directions: From I-5 in South Redding, take the Churn Creek Road or Bonnyview Road exit and travel west on Bonnyview. Across the Sacramento River, Bonnyview ends at Highway 273 (S. Market Street). Turn left and travel south on Highway 273, about one mile to Clear Creek Road. Turn right and choose any of four signed trailheads on the left along the road.

Piety Hill Loop (902')   4.3   M   *Oak woodland, views of creek canyon and Shasta Bolly*

The Clear Creek Greenway is perhaps the most unique location in the Redding area. With live oak and granite in profusion, it is more reminiscent of the Sierra foothills. It certainly offers the most beautiful hiking in the area. From the Horsetown parking area, cross Clear Creek Road to the trail signed, *To Cloverdale Trails*. The trail climbs immediately and rises across hillsides dotted with pink granite among foothill pine, blue oak, manzanita, and buckbrush. There is soon a dramatic view down into a deep and scenic gorge of Clear Creek. Hoofprints make it clear that horse people love this place, and it is not unusual to encounter riders on the trail.

At the Piety Hill Loop, turn right. The trail winds down into a side canyon and crosses a rocky creek bed, blanketed by wild grape-vines just upstream. Beyond this is a junction with a trail heading uphill to the left, which can be a possible return option. For now, keep to the right. At the next junction, about 1.5 miles from the trailhead, a spur trail drops to a rugged cliff-top point with an exceptional view. You look down into the rocky depths of Clear Creek's canyon, with beautiful Shasta Bally rising over pine-covered slopes beyond, as if anchored in an ancient Chinese painting.

Back on the loop, the trail continues up and away from the canyon into a live oak grove. Near the top, the path winds around the eastern brow of the hill, affording views across low ridges to the Sacramento Valley. You then traverse across the crest of Piety Hill, covered with manzanita in this location. A trail junction offers the option of the connector on the left, cutting down through the heart of the preserve for a shorter loop. Your route continues to the right. Just after cresting the hill, the trail briefly parallels an old, grass-covered ditch that once served the many mining operations located farther down Clear Creek.

Along the ridge, the trail winds along the route of an old road mostly vanished back into the grass. At the junction with the connector trail to the Cloverdale Loop, the Piety Hill Loop continues to the left, veering easterly for the return to the trailhead. The fence indicating Cloverdale Road becomes visible at the top of the slopes on your right. This is a level stretch of manzanita, with a grass-covered ditch paralleling the trail. At a junction, the midpreserve connector trail cuts to the left away from the road.

The Piety Hill Loop, on its downhill return to the trailhead, continues to parallel the road. It is worthwhile to take the connector trail, which first follows a ridge with extensive rock granite outcrops. Dropping into the heart of the preserve, you meet the other connector trail descending from the left. Turn right and gradually reach the rocky bottom of this side canyon. After a good rain, the creek bed fills with a pretty series of cascades. You soon reach the junction with the Piety Hill Loop. Turn right, and you are retracing your steps to the trailhead.

Directions: From I-5 in South Redding, take the Churn Creek Road or Bonnyview Road exit and travel west on Bonnyview. Across the Sacramento River, Bonnyview ends at Highway 273 (S. Market Street). Turn left and travel south on Highway 273, about one mile to Clear Creek Road. Turn right and follow Clear Creek Road, eight miles to the signed Horsetown parking area, on the left just past the bridge over Clear Creek.

Cloverdale Loop (910') 1.75 M *Oak woodland, views of creek canyon and Shasta Bolly*

Located in the western portion of Clear Creek Greenway, this trail is much less rugged than the Piety Hill Loop, with much elevation variation. Taking the left branch of the loop, the trail is a pleasant, packed-earth ramble across flat uplands covered with pine, blue oak, and manzanita. As the grassy slopes fall away, excellent views of Shasta Bally emerge.

Midway through this loop, a short spur trail cuts to the left to a vista point, farther upstream from the viewpoint on the Piety Hill Loop. Like that overlook, Cloverdale's vista point is a small. flat area with a picnic table and a rocky outcrop that offers an eagle-eye view of Clear Creek below. Shasta Bally dominates to the west. Tall foothill pines, with their unique twisting branches, spike the slopes all around. To be here in a nice breeze is pleasant, with the whispery rustle of the pine's sinuous limbs. Back on the main loop, continue back to the trailhead, passing the connector trail from the Piety Hill Loop.

Directions: From I-5 in South Redding, take the Churn Creek Road or Bonnyview Road exit and travel west on Bonnyview. Across the Sacramento River, Bonnyview ends at Highway 273 (S. Market Street). Turn left and travel south on Highway 273, about one mile to Clear Creek Road. Turn right and follow Clear Creek Road, past Clear Creek, to Cloverdale Road. Turn right and follow Cloverdale Road uphill to the parking area on the right for the Cloverdale Trailhead.

Sacramento River Bend Outstanding Natural Area. Also known as Paynes Creek Recreation Area, this region in Tehama County, northeast of Red Bluff, is composed mostly of rolling grasslands and oak woodlands, but there are also marshy wetlands, lava outcrops, and access to the Sacramento River. Miles of scenic trails offer solitude, since it is likely to meet more people on horseback than on foot.

Iron Canyon Loop (706') 3 M Volcanic plateau, rim walk, view of Sacramento River

This is a level loop on a sparsely vegetated, volcanic tableland. Though the scrub brush offers little shade, the views are great. The path from the parking area travels about fifty yards before dropping into a gully. Just beyond the gully, the trail splits for its loop. Either direction will bring you back to this point. In about one mile, the trail reaches the rim of a lava bluff high above the Iron Canyon section of the Sacramento River. This is the only place where lava–flows from Cascade Range eruptions reaches the river. Follow the rim north to where the trail veers away from the river to continue its loop back to the trailhead.

Directions: From Highway 99 at the east end of Red Bluff, take Highway 32 for 5.3 miles to the trailhead parking area on the left.

Hog Lake Plateau and Vista Trail (750') 1–8 E/M Grasslands, views, spring wildflowers

Hog Lake shimmers about a half mile northwest of the trailhead across an open savannah, but that's not the main reason for a walk here. Spring wildflowers and far-ranging vistas on a flat route is the appeal here. The four-mile hike to the Iron Canyon Vista Point is not the shortest route, but it is the driest, without the necessity of wading through Paynes Creek. The Paynes Creek Crossing trailhead is miles closer, but is more suitable for horses. From the trailhead, besides Hog Lake, you can spot Mt. Shasta dominating the north horizon. Southwest, the Yolla Bolly peaks are visible.

The snowy mounts of Lassen Peak and Broke-Off Mountain rise to the east, seemingly just beyond a stone's throw away. The trail is an old gravel ranch road across the treeless plateau. In 0.25 miles, just after crossing Turtle Creek, the drainage from Hog Lake, the trail turns south through the grassland, verdant in spring with yellow wildflowers highlighting vernal pools. On the right, blue oaks dot a small ridge that parallels the trail.

As you head south, Turtle Creek cuts its channel deeper into the plateau, oaks become more numerous, and snowcapped Snow Mountain appears far to the south in the Coast Range. The low bumps that are the Orland Buttes protrude from the valley floor, where it rolls into the western foothills. The trail winds to the west and begins to drop into the Paynes Creek watershed. To the northeast, Shasta Bally and the craggy Trinity Alps emerge. After descending from the plateau, cross a broad grassland. Where the old road drops into the wetlands, a slim white marker on the left indicates a narrow footpath taking off to the south.

This path, otherwise unmarked, is the Vista Trail. As the path wanders along the top of a grassy bluff, you can look down into the flat marshes and hear mixed birdsongs from below. Your path comes to a junction. A sign indicates "Scout" Trail straight ahead. This is an option for exploring the oak woodlands above what is now a gorge of Turtle Creek. Instead, turn right on the trace of an old ranch road. You soon reach another junction, the beginning of the loop. Either way works.

Taking the left fork, pass the lower end of the Scout Trail. Beyond that, Turtle Creek has become a serious chasm as it drops to meet the Sacramento River just ahead. The trail rounds a bend where the river and the rugged bluffs of Iron Canyon are visible, with the hump of Iron Mountain across the river. The trail skirts the top of river bluffs and lives up to its name, offering excellent views of the green river below, boulder-strewn bluffs, and homes of the Bend community upriver. As the trail winds away from the river, look down to where Paynes Creek flows out of the wetland that fills its small valley between a woodland of blue oak and gray pine. From this point, retrace your steps to the trailhead. One option for the return is to scramble to the top of the small ridge on the plateau and follow it as it parallels the trail to Hog Lake.

Directions: From Highway 99 at the east end of Red Bluff, take Highway 32 for 7.6 miles to the trailhead parking area on the left.

Paynes Creek Wetlands (331')   2   E   *Wetlands, birds, pond, river access*

Easy paths meander through marshy Pacific-Flyway wetlands to the east with good bird-watching, or around Bass Pond, west of the parking area, and down to the Sacramento River. This is also the southern end of the Yana Trail, which follows a route paralleling the river (but not riverside) to Massacre Flat and on to Jellys Ferry Bridge.

Directions: From I-5 north of Red Bluff, take Jellys Ferry Road east, 2.7 miles to Bend Ferry Road. Turn right and take Bend Ferry across the river and through the small community of Bend a few miles all the way to the natural area. The parking area is on the left not far beyond the area's entrance.

Coyote Pond (340')   1.5   E   *Pond, savannah, views*

From the parking area, follow the path through a small oak grove to an observation deck on the east shore of the pond. After appreciating the quietness of the pond, you can stroll on paths around the pond and beyond to the fringe of a grassy savannah that offers views of oak woodlands and Table Mountain across the river. There is no river access however.

Directions: From I-5 north of Red Bluff, take Jellys Ferry Road east, 2.7 miles to Bend Ferry Road. Turn right and take Bend Ferry across the river and through the small community of Bend a few miles all the way to the natural area. The turnoff for Coyote Pond is about two miles beyond the Bass Pond parking area.

Perry Riffle Trail (340') 2 E *Sacramento River access, oak woodland*

This is an easy meander on a loop that first samples the Sacramento River and then the valley woodland of oak and gray pine. Head north from the signed trailhead along the river for 0.75 miles. The trail then veers away from the river, offering a ramble up and over small, gentle ridges through the oak woodland that once covered most of the northern Sacramento Valley. At a trail junction, if you're not inclined to tackle a long hike to Massacre Flat upriver, turn right and amble back to the trailhead.

Directions: From I-5 north of Red Bluff, take Jellys Ferry Road east, 2.7 miles to Bend Ferry Road. Turn right and take Bend Ferry across the river and through the small community of Bend a few miles all the way to the natural area. The trailhead is at the road's end.

Osprey Pond (463') 1.5 E *Pond, views, spring wildflowers, good for kids*

Except for the very brief climb at the beginning, this is a pleasantly easy stroll with excellent views. From the trailhead, look for the single-track spur trail immediately on the left. Climb it—it's very brief—and then amble along, enjoying the expansive views of the surrounding countryside, which includes wildflowers in spring, Table Mountain across the Sacramento River to the south, and especially Lassen Peak rising grandly ahead of you to the east. Shade is sparse at the pond, just a couple of minimal trees. A loop is possible by continuing on the old ranch road past the pond's dam, down to the main path, and back to the trailhead, but it is perhaps more scenically satisfying to return the way you came, along the shallow ridge.

Directions: From I-5 north of Red Bluff, take Jellys Ferry Road east, to the trailhead signed as Oak Slough Trailhead, about a mile past the one-lane Jellys Ferry Bridge over the Sacramento River. The trailhead is on the right about one mile past the bridge.

Massacre Flat (576')   8   M   *Blue oak woodland, views of and access to Sacramento River*

Follow directions to Osprey Pond and continue past the pond to the main trail. Turn left and follow the old ranch road across a grassy savannah that dips into a dry creek bed and merges with the Yana Trail as the old road climbs to contour the upper slopes of a high river bluff. The Sacramento River flows below, the river full of rafts and fishermen on weekends. The trail drops into blue oak woodland and wanders away from the river, crosses Inks Creek and climbs to a grassy plateau.

Where the trail initially reaches the rim, a faint trail cuts to the right to a point with a great view of the river. Continuing along the plateau, a side trail drops to the right into a small canyon to Massacre Flat, an oak-shaded riverside area. Here you can rest next to the river and then retrace your steps to the trailhead. Massacre Flat can also be reached by the Yana Trail from Perry Riffle, but the trail is routed well away from the river. The Yana Trail has a trailhead at the Jellys Ferry Bridge, and the trail is near the river before it merges with the Oak Slough Trail.

Directions: From I-5 north of Red Bluff, take Jellys Ferry Road east, to the trailhead signed as Oak Slough Trailhead, about a mile past the one-lane Jellys Ferry Bridge over the Sacramento River. The trailhead is on the right about one mile past the bridge.

Whiskeytown Lake National Recreation Area
Brandy Creek Falls (2,500')   4   M   *Fir-oak forest, cascade waterfall, dogs on leash*

All the waterfalls in Whiskeytown NRA are located on the steep north slopes of Shasta Bally. Many consider Brandy Creek Falls to be the prettiest. From the trailhead, the trail immediately climbs steeply. A spur trail soon cuts down on the right to Brandy Creek. Continuing up, the main trail levels off after a half mile. In late summer / early autumn, the big leaf maples are in dazzling golden array.

After crossing a side creek on a wooden footbridge, the trail again rises sharply. The path is densely shaded, and sunlight at midday barely penetrates the thick forest cover. After another side canyon and a junction with the Rich Gulch Trail, ford a small stream on a sturdy wood plank and pass through a boggy area and a hillside stretch of large swordtail ferns. After a final uphill push, the trail levels off and arrives at a wooden bench and a view of Lower Brandy Creek Falls. The ten-foot cascade, framed by big-leaf maples, sweetly sets off the sublime peace of the spot.

The trail winds around and crosses above the falls, but any views are obscured by trees, and the slopes here are too precipitous for scrambling down. Metal railings are in place where the canyon narrows, and Brandy Creek spills downward in frothy cascades. At a wooden footbridge, Upper Falls are in sight, a white sheet through the maples. At this point, the trail becomes a scramble up rocks, with a footbridge visible at the top as a guide up the gorge beside fifty feet of very scenic cascades.

From that footbridge, another waterfall is visible upstream. The trail ends, and further approaches upstream require scrambling on river rocks. The return to the trailhead is pleasantly downhill.

Directions: From the Whiskeytown Visitor Center, take Kennedy Memorial Drive across the dam to Brandy Creek Beach. Turn left on Brandy Creek Road, unpaved but well-graded, and follow the signs 3.25 miles to the Brandy Creek Falls Trailhead.

Boulder Creek Falls (2,250') 2 M Fir-oak forest, waterfall, dogs on leash

From the Mill Creek Trailhead, it is one mile to the falls on an old forest road. Other than a brief steep pitch near the beginning, it is level going through manzanita, oak, pine, and some fir. After an easy ford across Boulder Creek, you meet the trail coming up from South Shore Drive. The falls are just ahead. A bench has been placed in a shaded nook for viewing the pretty cascade.

Next to this natural alcove, blocks have been embedded in the slope as stairs up to another viewpoint. Beyond this, a narrow, slope-hugging path traverses the mountainside to the thirty-foot upper cascade, not visible from below. Set in its rocky basin and framed by trees, ferns, and a fringe of green lushness, broad rocks just below the uppermost cascade make an excellent spot for sitting and savoring this pretty corner of the world.

Directions: From Highway 299 at the western end of Whiskeytown Lake, turn left on Carr Powerhouse Road. There is a lower trailhead along South Shore Drive, accessible from either end of Whiskeytown Lake; a hike from here is 5.5 miles round trip, half of which is an uphill climb. For a shorter walk, your vehicle can do the climbing on insanely steep and unpaved Mill Creek Road, a right turn on Carr Powerhouse Road one-half mile from Highway 299. It is 1.7 miles of mostly precipitous grade to the trailhead. It is well-graded, but narrow. Make sure your brakes are in good working order for the return descent.

Whiskeytown Falls (3,000')   3.4   M   *Fir-oak forest, waterfall, dogs on leash*

This spectacular waterfall was unknown to all but a few park rangers, until 2004 when it was sighted from the air by a park biologist. Although the route to the falls is a mostly uphill push, the trail begins in downhill mode briefly on a restored logging road. After a footbridge across Crystal Creek's west fork, the trail begins its gradual ascent through a pleasant woodland of firs, pines, and incense cedars.

At the trail junction, take the James K Carr Trail. There is a strenuous-for-some climb through a fern-thick section known as Steep Ravine. After leveling out and providing views at Wintu View, the trail narrows at Trail Camp. Horses and bicycles must be left here. The trail crosses a footbridge and enters a box canyon. The falls are a quarter mile farther. Here is a humid environment of ferns, mosses, and big-leaf maples.

At the falls, stone stairs to the left, with metal railings for safety on the slippery steps, allow access to the upper cascades at Photographer's Ledge and, higher still, at Artist's Ledge. Retrace your steps to the trailhead. Another worthwhile waterfall is easily accessible partway down Crystal Creek Road, at Crystal Creek Falls (elev. 1700'). This is barely a walk at 0.3 miles, but these spectacular cascades merit stretching your legs even a little bit.

Directions: From Highway 299, one mile past Carr Powerhouse Road, turn left on Crystal Creek Road. Drive uphill for 3.7 miles to the Mill Creek Trailhead. If you reach the Crystal Creek Conservation Center, you've gone too far. The marked turnoff for Crystal Creek Falls is about 1.5 miles below the Mill Creek Trailhead.

***Southern Cascades**—This is the land of volcanism, of bubbling mud pots, and lava tubes. From the Sacramento Valley, the summits of Shasta and Lassen are visible, their volcanic cones rising like snow-capped sentinels above the surrounding mountains. Most of the trails of the Southern Cascades are found in close proximity to one or the other of these peaks. Given its southerly latitudes, the vegetation has more in common with the North Sierra than the lush growth farther north in Oregon.*

Tehama Wildlife Area
McClure Trail

Lower Deer Creek Falls

Lassen Volcanic National Park
Brokeoff Mountain
Mill Creek Falls
Ridge Lakes
Bumpass Hell
Lassen Peak
Cliff, Shadow, Terrace Lakes
Kings Creek Falls
Chaos Crags
Lily Pond / Reflection Lake
Devils Kitchen
Boiling Lake / Terminal Geyser
Cinder Cone
Prospect Peak

Caribou Wilderness
Hidden Lakes Loop

Subway Cave
Burney Falls

Mt. Shasta Area
Castle Crags
McCloud River Falls
Black Butte

Castle / Heart Lakes

Devils Kitchen

Tehama Wildlife Area—This cascade foothill wildlife area is managed for wildlife preservation, chiefly for the winter herds of black-tailed deer, which make the longest migration of any herd on the Sierra West Slope. Wild turkeys and feral pigs also roam here. Two plant communities mingle here, blue oaks with black oaks and ponderosa pine with gray pine. The trail is actually mostly on adjacent national forest land, but access is through the wildlife area.

McClure Trail (3,500')   2-9   M   *Antelope Creek Canyon*

A small metal sign with a hiker icon is the only indication of the trailhead. The trail leaves the saddle and follows a seasonal creek drainage through a dense blue oak woodland. You descend gradually for 0.25 miles, and then the trail takes a steep dive into a small canyon. Patches of yellow star thistle along the path make long pants a recommendation. Rattlesnakes and, to a lesser extent, mountain lions are another reality, and caution should always be exercised if small children or dogs are present. After another 0.25 miles, the small canyon widens and joins the more expansive canyon of Antelope Creek's north fork. After crossing the side canyon on a switchback, the trail proceeds easterly across the slope of the main canyon. The panorama is extensive up and down the canyon. Resembling a greener Grand Canyon, the tiered strata formed by ancient lava flows are noticeably different from granite-studded Sierra foothills. The trail switchbacks and drops gradually to Antelope Creek within the wildlife area and continues along the creek to its end at Ishi Road. Use of the wildlife area is heavy only during hunting season (September 19–November 1), and solitude is prevalent the rest of the year.

Directions: From Highway 99 (Antelope Blvd) in Red Bluff, three miles east of I-5, take Highway 36 21 miles to the hamlet of Paynes Creek. Turn right on Paynes Creek Road. Just past the market, turn right on Plum Creek Road, which enters the wildlife area, winding up and along Plum Creek Ridge. At three miles from Highway 20, a right turn on High Trestle Road is two miles from the trailhead. High Trestle Road is initially well-graded gravel, but beyond a cattle guard becomes rocky, deeply-rutted, and rugged. The less risky option is to continue 2.5 miles farther on Plum Creek Road to Hogsback Road and turn right to the trailhead. Hogsback Road is unpaved but well-graded and follows the crest of Hogsback Ridge, providing outstanding views. The trailhead is in a saddle at the junction of Hogsback and High Trestle roads.

Lower Deer Creek Falls (3,600')   4.6   E   *Deer Creek, waterfall*

Deer Creek is one of the prettiest streams in the state. It flows from its headwaters on Butt Mountain eighty-eight miles to the Sacramento River, through forested mountains, and then the lava canyons of the Ishi Wilderness before languidly crossing the valley floor to join the river near Vina. The trail to Lower Deer Creek Falls begins across Highway 32, closer to the highway bridge.

A level path with gentle ups and downs, it is pleasantly shaded, with occasional open views upslope of lava pinnacles and crags. The trees are a mix of ponderosa pine, live oak, incense cedar, canyon oak, and Douglas fir. Be alert for poison oak along the trail. You are never out of sight or sound of Deer Creek, but you are generally routed across the slopes above the stream, sometimes at a considerable distance. You are approaching the falls when the trail leaves the shade and climbs across an open slope with a view down the canyon.

The top of the falls is visible at this point. The falls are a long cataract, dropping through a small rocky gorge. At the bottom, the biggest plunge, a twenty-foot drop, is best viewed from a large promontory jutting out into the middle of the creek. It is easily accessed by a spur trail descending from the main trail. A second spur trail leads to the fish ladder constructed around the falls. Retrace your steps to the trailhead. To reach Upper Deer Creek Falls, four miles farther upstream from the Lower Falls trailhead, start at the signed pull-off on the highway. A short, steep path drops about one hundred feet to rocky shelves with excellent views of Upper Falls. This is a plunge type of waterfall into a small punchbowl formation. There is viewing space for a good amount of people; the limited parking space will keep Upper Falls from being too crowded.

Directions: Take Highway 32 from Chico up into the mountains. At forty-one miles, the Lower Falls trailhead is on the right, just after crossing Deer Creek. The Upper Falls is four miles farther, adjacent to the road on the right.

Lassen Volcanic National Park—California's own Yellowstone is a land of steam vents, mud pots, and volcanic aftermath. Some of the most beautiful hikes in Northern California are found here, but even at the peak of summer, lack the crowds of Yosemite and Tahoe. Though the main road through the park is closed to vehicles in winter, it is open for snow activities. Dogs are prohibited on all trails within the national park.

Brokeoff Mountain (9,235') 7.4 M/SC *Fir forest, views of Sacramento Valley and Mt. Tehama's base*

This is the most beautiful path and best hike in the park. Lassen Peak is justifiably the centerpiece, but Brokeoff Mountain offers better views, including a sublime panorama of ancient Mt. Tehama's core. Brokeoff Mountain is the most prominent remnant of the once eleven-thousand-foot Shasta-like volcano. (The still-steaming thermal heart of the old mountain is still evident in the vicinity of the roadside Sulphur Works, a mile north of the visitor center.) The Brokeoff trailhead has no great portal to welcome you. You merely cross the highway and plunge into a gap in the low foliage.

The trail promptly rises and, with few exceptions, will continue that way to the summit. You will definitely earn this hike, with a 2,600-foot elevation gain in 3.6 miles. Beyond an alder thicket, you climb through a fir forest, with glimpses of surrounding peaks through the trees. Where the tree levels off, boulders to the left are evidence of impressive rock slides. The trail also parallels the outlet creek from Forest Lake. After a bit of steepness, the trail levels off again, and a side trail to the left heads about fifty yards to a mostly grassy, wet meadow. Farther up the main trail is a lupine-ringed meadow, where the creek flows through separated into glassy pools by sinuous mounds of long-tufted grass. At this point, Brokeoff Mountain looms before you with a lot of elevation yet to gain.

Continuing on, you encounter a junction with the blocked-off 0.25-mile side trail to Forest Lake. This small lake is snag-ridden and offers neither swimming, fishing, or camping. After crossing the outlet creek on muddy banks and soggy planks, the trail proceeds uphill, away from the small stream, and begins to make serious elevation. Distant ridges emerge, and another old rockfall mutely testifies to the volatile nature of this landscape. White firs give way to red firs, and Lake Almanor pops into view to the southeast.

Always there are nearby peaks in their primeval ruggedness. A short side trail to the right cuts over to a rim with a view of weedy Forest Lake one hundred feet below. Approaching the base of the peak, the trail traverses a massive rockfall, clearly part of what "broke off" its starkness, softened by vivid-yellow balsamroot blooming among the boulders. There are long switchbacks ahead, and you will become more aware of the altitude. The air is thinner, and the firs are sparser. Childs Meadow and the gray ribbon of Highway 89 become visible. The trail rounds a bend on a spur ridge, and there are your first views of the Sacramento Valley and the Coast Range.

Now the trail crosses a mostly open slope, always climbing. The vista is extraordinary: To the west are the Yolla Bollys, with Snow Mountain fifty miles south in the Coast Range. Directly south are the clefts cut into the foothills by Antelope and Mill creeks. Far to the south, the Sutter Buttes poke up from the flat valley floor. At the final switchback before the summit, an unsigned trail heads west down the ridge, out of the park to Heart Lake.

Moving on, the trail's final leg does not ease its grade until a saddle just below the peak, and then it is an easy fifty feet to the relatively flat summit. The view is possibly more breathtaking than that from Lassen's summit, 1,200 feet higher. Perhaps it is the vantage point, looking north along the ridge that stretches spectacularly to Lassen. Lower are the peach-colored hues of mineral deposits, pastel shades of hydrothermal activities scattered across the slopes in Little Hot Springs Valley and the Sulphur Works below. It almost seems beside the point to mention that Mt. Shasta, to the northwest, seems startlingly close. The bonus of this hike comes with the return descent, an easy downhill that allows for enjoyment of a variety of panoramas.

Directions: Take Highway 36 east from Red Bluff, then Highway 89 north (for a total of fifty-three miles) to the trailhead, located on the right one-half mile past the national park boundary, but before the entry station. There is a self-pay facility at the pullout.

Mill Creek Falls (6,725')　3.2　M　*Forest, wildflowers (mule's ears), waterfall*

Mill Creek Falls is considered the most picturesque of the few waterfalls in the park. The relatively easy 1.6-mile trail begins just below the visitor center amphitheater at the northeast corner of the parking area. The path winds down through a shaded white fir forest to a wooden footbridge across West Sulphur Creek. It then traverses across an open slope covered with mule's ears, spectacular with yellow blossoms through most of the summer. The trail winds into a forest cover and then drops about three hundred feet before heading back up in a steady climb for about 0.25 miles. You will hear the falls before you see them.

With a drop totaling seventy-five feet, it is visible from a viewpoint across the canyon. The impressive waterfall really consists of two streams, East Sulphur Creek from Little Hot Springs Valley and Bumpass Creek from Bumpass Hell, falling together into one pool and then farther as one long drop. Two footbridges cross the streams just above the falls, where you get a close look at the lip at the top. It is impossible (or at least impractical) to try to get to the base of the falls. For the best photo opportunities, view the falls between noon and midafternoon, to catch optimal sunlight in the narrow canyon.

Directions: Trailhead is on main Park Road (Highway 89) just inside the south entrance station, at the Kohm Yah-mah-nee Visitor Center.

Ridge Lakes (8,000')   2   SC   *Sulphur Works, lakes*

At only a mile on the map from the trailhead to the small lakes tucked under the ridge that extends from Brokeoff Mountain to Lassen Peak, this might be the shortest trail in the park. But it is also possibly the steepest one mile in Northern California (with the exception of the Castle Crags Trail.) From the trailhead, signed clearly for Ridge Lakes, the trail starts its ascent immediately. The trail builders here opted for the Alpine style, which means not even a hint of switchbacks from start to finish.

Fortunately, the scenery and expanding views go a long way as compensation for the workout. The first part of the trail follows a narrow ridge up an old landslide that has stabilized between two creeks. On the right is West Sulphur Creek. Bubbling turquoise pools are visible at accessible viewpoints. Wafts of the nose-wrinkling odor of sulfur remind you that you are on no ordinary forest path. The creeks emerge from springs in small clearings that are brilliant with wildflowers in Lassen's short summer.

For the final 0.25 miles, the trail becomes absurdly steep. Walking sticks are advised for this hike. The lakes are really one lake with a narrow isthmus in the middle. It sits in a nearly treeless bowl. The ridge above marks the flanks of ancient Mt. Tehama, the volcanic giant that would match Mt. Shasta in massiveness if the ancestral mountain hadn't exploded. Mt. Dillard looms craggily to the north. The formal trail ends at the lake, but it is possible to hoof it up the open slopes to the ridgeline for views of the Coast Range and Mt. Shasta. When done enjoying the serenity of the dramatic setting (no surprise, fewer people are found on this trail than any other on Highway 89), return the way you came. It is a much quicker trip than the trudge up.

Directions: Trailhead is on main Park Road (Highway 89) at the Sulphur Works parking area, one mile past visitor center.

Bumpass Hell (8,450')   3   M   *Views, boiling mud pots, good for kids*

This is perhaps the most popular trail in the park, and it is a good introduction to the special features that sets this park apart from anywhere in California. Keep in mind that snow melts here later than other mountain regions. In July, after a heavy winter, snow can still be a foot deep on the trail. From the trailhead, the route is level, gradually climbing as it contours along Bumpass Mountain, providing great views southward of the Mill Creek watershed. After reaching a gap, it is about 0.5 miles down into the vale of steaming mud pots that is Bumpass Hell.

A sturdy wooden boardwalk ensures that no one accidentally steps through the thin crust and suffers severe burns or worse. Besides the acres of bubbling natural cauldrons, clouds of steam hiss from the ground, a surface colored in pastel hues of pink, yellow, coral, and off-white, devoid of any vegetation.

Named for an early settler who accidentally stepped into the scalding mud and promptly gave the place its moniker, its initial otherworldliness makes it endlessly fascinating—until the sulfuric reek hits your nose. The odor pervades the place and usually proves to be the limiting factor in how long anyone lingers here. Cold Boiling Lake is about a mile beyond Bumpass Hell, and if a shuttle is arranged, you can continue there and then on by way of Mill Creek Falls to the Southwest Visitor Center. Otherwise, retrace your steps to the trailhead.

Directions: Trailhead is on the main park road (Highway 89), six miles from the Southwest Visitor Center and one mile south of the Lassen Peak trailhead parking. The trailhead parking area has an excellent view of Little Hot Springs Valley.

Lassen Peak (10,457')   5   SC   *Volcanic crater, views of all surrounding area*

This is, of course, the centerpiece hike in the park. Though it's only 2.5 miles to the summit, anyone who thinks they can just charge up the trail to the top is likely to pep-step right into altitude sickness. The trailhead is already over eight thousand feet elevation and climbs two thousand feet in two miles. One of Mt. Lassen's remarkable features is that a well-graded footpath provides relatively easy access to the peak, and there are not many places where one can "stroll" to the top of a 10,457-foot mountain.

It's probably a good idea to take this trail slowly. The path is very distinct. If there is still snow at the trailhead, small flags placed in the snow will keep you headed in the right direction. Even without the flags, the steady stream of hikers in both directions will keep you on track. Without snow, the trail is rocky, having been carved out of the volcanic cone. For those with children or who have a problem with heights, the trail isn't too precarious, as the view grows more expansive with every step. Like an organic StairMaster, every step is in an uphill mode. Frequent rests make it possible to pause and savor the spreading panorama.

To the south, Lake Almanor is a gleaming blue expanse, and beyond are Spanish Peak and the North Sierra escarpment of the Bucks Lake Wilderness. Southwest the bumps of the Sutter Buttes rise out of the haze, incongruous with the flatness of the surrounding Sacramento Valley. At the summit, you may wander around the once-explosive crater. The view is tremendous in every direction. Mt. Shasta looms to the northwest like an older sibling. When ready to descend (and it is a descent all the way back), return the way you came.

Directions: Trailhead is on the main park road (Highway 89), nine miles from the Southwest Visitor Center.

Cliff, Shadow, Terrace Lakes (8,050') 3.5 M *Fir forest, scenic lakes*

These three very picturesque lakes are close enough to each other to allow a leisurely visit at each lake. From the road, the trail descends and keeps descending, meaning a return climb. Due to its location in a sub-alpine zone, the upper part of the trail can be snow-covered until mid-July. A quarter mile down, at the junction with the trail to

Paradise Meadows, veer right to Terrace Lake. In a forest of hemlocks and firs, Terrace Lake is scenically set against a rocky bluff. Set in a lightly forested basin, 0.02 miles farther to the east and a bit lower, Shadow Lake is a remarkable blue-green. The trail descends to the lake and follows the east shore.

From this vantage, Lassen Peak now looms to the west. Continuing to Cliff Lake, the trail leaves Shadow Lake and heads east in a pleasant ramble, making a very gradual descent through rocky meadows and old-growth firs. The junction with the short spur trail to Cliff Lake is one mile from Terrace Lake. Of the three lakes, Cliff Lake is easily in the most spectacular setting. Appropriately named, it sits at the base of Reading Peak. A massive wall of rock rises above the boulder-strewn rubble that forms the lake's south shore. Instead of returning to the trailhead, one option is to continue 2.2 miles farther from Cliff Lake to Summit Lake on the park road. Another option is to head down the Paradise Meadows Trail; from the trail junction, Paradise Meadows is 1.0 mile down and 1.5 miles farther to the Hat-Creek trailhead.

Directions: Trailhead is at Roadside Marker 27 on the main Park Road (Highway 89), 9.7 miles from the south park boundary and two miles east of the Lassen Peak Trailhead.

Kings Creek Falls (7,285')　2.7　M　*Fir forest, cascade waterfall*

Mill Creek Falls may be more dramatic, but Kings Creek Falls is by far prettier. For the first half mile, the trail descends gradually along the creek through shaded forest to Lower Kings Creek Meadow. Pass the trail junction were the Sifford Lake trail cuts off to the right. About 0.25 miles farther, at the top of Kings Creek Cascades, there is an option of routes. I recommend taking the left choice, the gentler and 0.3 miles longer horse trail, and return by the steeper Cascades trail. The two trails rejoin seven hundred feet lower, at the bottom of the narrow gorge. Continue on the trail about a third of a mile to the falls. A fenced overlook provides an excellent view of the waterfall. The National Park Service measures the falls at thirty feet, but other accounts suggest that it is forty to fifty feet high. The waterfall sports mist-loving ferns and moss that thrive in the spray. For the best photos, time your visit before noon, when the falls become shaded.

Return by way of the Cascade Trail instead of the horse trail, up to a steep stone staircase constructed beside Kings Creek, with great views of the trailside cascades. Depending on the volume of water, the stone steps may be slippery in the spray. (Think of the Mist Trail in Yosemite.)

Note the bent red firs on this hike. Due to the heavy snowfall that the Lassen area receives every winter, these trees are warped into bent curves by the immense weight of the snowpack.

Directions: Trailhead is on the main park road (Highway 89), about halfway (sixteen miles) between the north and south entrances of the national park.

Chaos Crags (6,630') 4 M *Manzanita Lake, forest, views of Chaos Jumbles and Crags*

At 5,900 feet, the Manzanita Lake area is the lowest altitude along the main Park Road and is snow-free earlier. Chaos Crags are a series of dacite volcanoes that pushed up as lava plugs 1,200 years ago. Trail makes a gradual ascent from the trailhead through a dense Jeffrey pine forest. Unseen, Manzanita Creek parallels the trail on the right. The trail travels up and away from the creek, skirting an ancient glacial moraine.

Away from traffic, the stillness is punctuated with the sounds of birds and wind through the trees. The path climbs onto a moraine, and the forest thins out. The next 0.25 mile is charred by a past forest fire, and shade is scant. Beyond this is an open slope covered with scrubby pinemat manzanita. The spiky pinnacles of Chaos Crags loom ahead. The trail formally ends at the Chaos Jumbles, the rocky and desolate remnant of a massive landslide. The three avalanches that created the Jumbles happened in quick succession about three hundred years ago. A primitive trail continues down into the depression of Chaos Crater where tiny Crags Lake sits. Snow-fed, it is barely a pond in summer.

Directions: Trailhead is off main Park Road (Highway 89). A half mile from the north entrance station, heading into the park, turn right just past the Loomis Museum onto the road to Manzanita Lake Campground. Trailhead is on the left, 0.25 miles down the road.

Lily Pond / Reflection Lake (5,900')   1.5   E   *Fir forest, lakes*

This easy stroll in the forest takes in a group of small, scenic lakes. The trail begins across the road from the Loomis-Museum parking area. Heading clockwise, you first circle Reflection Lake, which sits adjacent to the road. The trail then heads deeper into the forest and circles Lily Pond, which lives up to its name as much of the pond's surface is covered with disc-like lily pads. The loop trail reemerges at the park road and your vehicle.

Directions: Trailhead is located across main Park Road (Highway 89) from Loomis Museum, less than a half mile into the park from the north entrance station.

Devils Kitchen (6,020')   5   M   *Fir forest, boiling mud pots*

The Drakesbad vicinity is where you can find the greatest concentration of different varieties of thermal features. This can be combined with the following trail for a long loop. A short distance from the trailhead, the trail passes over a wet meadow on planks and crosses Hot Spring Creek. You climb and cross an open hillside, where small creeks babble downward to the resort below. Being out-lets from thermal springs, the water is very hot. Beyond this is a trail junction, left for Boiling Springs Lake, and your choice, right for Devils Kitchen. Pass the closed trail to Dream Lake and cross Hot Springs Creek again.

After passing the access trail from Drakesbad, thread through the trees at the edge of broad Upper Meadow, also referred to as Hot Spring Valley. Beyond a plank walkway across a soggy portion of the meadow, the trail heads up the middle of the valley. At the western edge of the long meadow, the trail enters a dense white fir forest. When you encounter a hitching rail for horses, you've arrived.

A brief trail descends to the Devils Kitchen basin, where steam curls up from the multihued landscape. Cross the creek by footbridge for the short loop. (Despite the name, Hot Spring Creek is as icy cold as any mountain stream.)

Along the loop, steam emerges from the bare ground. Do not approach these vents; the surrounding crust may be thin, and someone could unexpectedly be plunged into a scalding morass. Out in the pink-and-chalk-colored basin, you can see the furiously boiling mud pots. Their gurgles and plops are audible above the rush of the creek. The upper leg of the loop winds directly beside vents and mud pots. White clouds of steam drift constantly across the path. The plop from belching mud provides a unique soundtrack, like free-form percussion. Retrace your steps toward Drakesbad. Mt. Harkness is visible where it anchors the eastern end of Warner Valley.

Directions: From Chester on Highway 36 near Lake Almanor, take Feather River Road, signed for Drakesbad and Juniper Lake. Within a few blocks, take the left fork for Drakesbad. A few miles farther, turn right on Warner Valley Road. Just before reaching the park boundary, the pavement ends, and the final three miles are well-graded gravel. It is self-pay at the ranger station. The trailhead is on the left, just past the Warner Valley Campground and 0.25 miles before Drakesbad. Unless you are a guest at the resort, park here.

Boiling Springs Lake / Terminal Geyser (6,250') 4.2 M *Fir forest, steaming lake, huge steam vent*

See previous entry for Devils Kitchen for directions to this point. From the junction with the Devils Kitchen trail, turn left on the Boiling Springs Lake Trail. It is a half mile gradually uphill through forest to the lake, which lives up to its name. Steam rises from the jade-colored water, which has been measured at 125 degrees. Along the more open west side of the lake, you can see mud pots along the shore, bubbling like overheated oatmeal.

Across the lake's south end lies a broad shelf of boiling, steaming mud pots; these are the springs that feed the lake. The trail loops around the lake. The signed trail to Terminal Geyser, 2.3 miles farther, takes off from the south loop and climbs steadily, but not too strenuously, through a forested landscape. After a half mile, the trail first levels and then begins a gradual descent through dense forest. At the junction with the Pacific Crest Trail, you can see white puffs of steam at a short distance through the trees.

From here, follow the signs to Terminal Geyser. The route drops steeply if briefly and then winds into the canyon on an abandoned use-road. This was a private inholding before 1980, when the park service took it into the park. Terminal Geyser is an immense steam vent. Vast clouds of steam continually spew upwards to fifty feet and higher. It sounds like a small blast furnace embedded in large boulders at the base of a high bluff. A scalding-hot boiling creek bubbles out of the rocks and flows downslope. There are no fences or boardwalks here, so use caution when scrambling for a closer look. In returning to the trailhead, you have the option of retracing your steps to Boiling Springs Lake or taking the Pacific Crest Trail; the distance is the same.

Directions: From Chester on Highway 36 near Lake Almanor, take Feather River Road, signed for Drakesbad and Juniper Lake. Within a few blocks, take the left fork for Drakesbad. A few miles farther, turn right on Warner Valley Road. Just before reaching the park boundary, the pavement ends, and the final three miles are well-graded gravel. It is self-pay at the ranger station. The trailhead is on the left, just past the Warner Valley Campground and 0.25 miles before Drakesbad. Unless you are a guest at the resort, park here.

Cinder Cone (6,907') 4 M/SC *Volcanic cone, lava beds, ash dunes, views*

This remote corner of the park offers another unique experience of volcanism's effects. Your route is on the historic Nobles Emigrant Trail, broad enough for covered wagons and level in a rolling way. The path is cinder-covered and can be akin to walking on a beach. To the left stretch the volcanic debris of the Fantastic Lava Beds, the solidified "ripples" of a former lava flow.

At almost a half mile, the Prospect Peak Trail cuts off to the right. Continue past this junction as the trail climbs away from the black jumbles of the lava bed onto the cinder fields. Cinder Cone begins to loom ahead through the trees. As you near it, the trail snaking up its precipitous slope becomes visible. 1.2 miles from the trailhead, the side trail to the cone forks to the left. From here you can make the slow, steady climb to Cinder Cone's summit crater, or continue on the Emigrant Trail for a fine view of the Painted Dunes beyond the lava beds. The trail to the summit is dependably steep, with loose rock every step of the way. It is wide enough that those who have issues with heights can walk away from the trail's edge.

At the top, it is easy to circumnavigate the crater, and a steep trail descends into its heart. The view is exceptional, encompassing Lassen Peak across the park and the lava beds / painted dunes below. After exploring the summit, you can take an optional trail down the back of Cinder Cone for a close-up view of the dunes and the vent at the cone's base from which the original lava beds spewed. This side trail reconnects with the Emigrant Trail for the return to the trailhead.

Directions: From Highway 44 between Hat Creek and Susanville, take Forest Road 32N21, signed for Butte Lake. It is six miles, unpaved with gravel, wide and well-graded, very manageable by passenger vehicle. Park at the end of the road, at the Butte Lake trailhead for Cinder Cone.

Prospect Peak (8,338')   6.6   M   *Fir forest, views from summit*

Follow the directions for the previous hike to Cinder Cone. At the junction with the signed Prospect Peak Trail, at 0.4 miles on the right, take that trail. The trail starts climbing immediately. A cindery trail surface does not make for quick progress. You are walking through an open area of Jeffrey pines, with zero undergrowth. The forest floor is a coat of pine needles, pinecones, and random fallen trees. The trail was constructed in the alpine manner—directly up the slope, with little semblance of switchbacks.

As you make elevation, scrub manzanita appears and becomes a broader carpet across the slopes. The pines transition to all fir, and volcanic rubble from past eruptions protrude into the landscape. As you near the summit, the trail's pitch steepens into semi-switchbacks. Through the trees, there are glimpses of Cinder Cone, Snag Lake, and the eastern reaches of the park. Near the east summit, the trail rounds a bend and Lassen Peak is visible, the master of this domain. At the top, the summit is broad and open. The trail continues another half mile to the west summit. The view is as spectacular as one would expect, including much of the park plus Mt. Shasta to the northwest. On the much quicker descent, you may encounter the scolding chirps of ground squirrels.

Directions: From Highway 44 between Hat Creek and Susanville, take Forest Road 32N21, signed for Butte Lake. It is six miles, unpaved with gravel, wide and well-graded, very manageable by passenger vehicle. Park at the end of the road, at the Butte Lake trailhead for Cinder Cone.

Caribou Wilderness—Adjoining Lassen National Park, there has never been caribou here; what you'll find here are a number of small, scenic lakes and quiet, walking through an exceptionally pretty forest landscape, easily accessed from Highway 36 near Lake Almanor.

Hidden Lakes Loop (6,880')　　5　　M　　*Fir forest, meadows, scenic lakes*

This is a very pretty forest walk on a gently climbing trail. The trail heads north, skirting Hay Meadow, and veers into a forest of fir and Jeffrey pine, soon reaching the wilderness boundary. Shortly beyond is the junction with the Hidden Lakes Trail. This is the beginning of the loop and can be done in either direction, but clockwise is gentler. On the trail to Beauty Lake, you travel on the south edge of Indian Meadow. A pond at the lower end of the meadows is covered with floating flat lily pads.

In this relatively flat wilderness, strenuous climbing is rare. In midsummer, wildflowers line the trail, which also signifies hordes of mosquitoes at every pause. At the junction with the trail to Long

Lake, continue on the left to Beauty Lake. That lake is ironically named, as it is possibly the least scenic lake on this loop. Beauty Lake is forested to its steep shore, with no level spots near the water. The trail threads through the trees along the south shore then heads up and away for a short distance to Evelyn Lake.

With its upper and lower lakes and rocky western shore, Evelyn Lake is a very scenic spot for resting or camping. From here, the trail heads north to Posey Lake. Tree-ringed and grassy banked, Posey Lake is large and accessible. The trail swings around the lake and drops slightly to the junction of trails at the south end of Long Lake. The left-hand option is the trail north to other trailheads. To continue your loop, turn right to Hidden Lakes. Pass the trail on the right, which returns you to the trailhead, and head on to Hidden Lakes.

The trail veers to the south and begins to pass the series of small lakes. Hidden Lakes are little more than picturesque ponds, lakelets if you will, tucked into the forest. Beyond Lake 5, the trail drops steeply and is why this route is done in this direction. At the bottom of the steep descent is a pretty, green meadow with corn lilies. Very shortly the trail is skirting the eastern edge of Indian Meadow. When there's a breeze, the bright green meadow ripples like an emerald sea. The trail soon reaches the junction with the route back to the trailhead and the end of the loop.

Directions: From Highway 36 east of Chester, where County Road A-13 is on the right for Lake Almanor, turn left for a short distance to a junction with New Chester Dump Road. Turn left and then a quick right onto Forest Road 10. Travel on the paved road for ten miles and turn left at the road signed for Caribou Wilderness. This forest road is unpaved and rough for 1.5 miles, but is manageable for passenger cars. The trailhead has parking for many vehicles.

Subway Cave (4,350') 0.5 E Lava tube, flashlight necessary, good for kids

In spite of its very short length, Subway Cave is an unforgettable adventure. Arm with a good flashlight and a thick headpiece to avoid knocking your scalp on the sometimes-low cave ceiling. Shoes are also advised because the cave floor, though seeming flat as an empty room, is uneven and calls for proceeding somewhat slowly through the lava tube. Because it is several degrees cooler underground, a sweatshirt or light jacket might be appreciated. From the parking area, a short path winds through the brush of the Hat Creek Valley to Subway Cave's entrance. Continue down the stairs into the lava tube. Turning on flashlights, proceed into the darkness.

Though only 0.25 miles in length, it will be completely dark not too far inside. The tube is residue from the volcanic activity, which has shaped this entire region over many centuries. A side chamber invites exploring. Before you know it, you round a bend, and there's the silhouette of the exit stairs. On the short return path to the parking area, you can muse on the fact that similar tubes snake beneath the brush and ground cover of the area.

Directions: Subway Cave is located on Highway 89, just north of the junction with Highway 44, and just north of the small community of Old Station. From the highway junction, Highway 89 combines with Highway 44 for about fifteen miles to the north entrance for Lassen National Park, where Highway 89 heads south through the park, and Highway 44 heads west to Redding. A restroom is available at the trailhead.

Burney Falls (3,281')   1.3   E   *Waterfall*

Located in Burney Falls Memorial State Park, 129-foot Burney Falls, though not the highest waterfall in the state, is certainly one of the most ethereally pretty. In this volcanic region, basalt is the underlying bedrock. Rain and snowmelt collect underground and emerge as springs into Burney Creek, as well as into the waterfall itself. Due to the plentiful water in the porous rock, the falls run all year, even in California's arid bone-dry summer.

The 1.3 miles Falls Loop Trail begins at an overlook, then descends into the small canyon cut by Burney Creek. The trail reaches the bottom of the waterfall and offers a spectacular view of the roaring main falls backed by the lacelike curtain of fairy-delicate cascades streaming from underground springs. The loop returns via short switchbacks up to the rim and concludes at the overlook. There is an entry fee, and dogs are not permitted on the trail. A very popular park, it is best to arrive in the early morning.

Directions: Take Highway 299 northeast from Redding. At the small town of Burney, turn left (north) on Highway 89 and travel six miles to the park.

Mount Shasta Area—an hour north of Redding, Mt. Shasta is never far out of view on any of its nearby trails.

Castle Crags (4,966') 5.4 SC *Granite domes, view of Mt. Shasta, no dogs*

This is easily the steepest trail in this guide, step for step. On no other trail will you be looking so "upward" as opposed to "ahead." These eye-catching pinnacles are familiar to anyone who has driven up or down I-5 between California and Oregon. Aptly named, the small jagged ridge rises above the dark-green forest like an ancient fortress. The trail is deceptively level for the shaded first 0.25 miles to the junction with the Root Creek Trail, which heads down to the right. The Castle Crags Trail climbs to the left, and up you go.

After crossing the Pacific Crest Trail, you switchback up to an open ridge with the first excellent view of Castle Crags above. The trail traverses this ridge at a less severe grade. At the junction with the Indian Springs Trail, it is 0.2 miles on that spur trail to water. Beyond this junction, your route upward renews its strictly steep ascent. At the wilderness boundary, views of Mt. Shasta emerge. A few switchbacks later, you reach the granite outcrops that signify the lower reaches of the crags. From here the trees thin out, and the trail leaves packed earth behind to climb open rocky slopes.

The final 0.75 miles is as rugged as they come. It can be easy to miss switchbacks, as the path is less a trail and more about scrambling across a rocky surface. Approaching the top, the trail diverges into rock-climber trails into the scrubby manzanita. At the crest, in a saddle below Castle Dome, you can spend hours wandering among the granite, savoring the views before making seemingly quick descent to the trailhead. It is possible to continue into the upper Crags, but that requires technical rock-climbing experience.

Directions: From I-5 just south of Dunsmuir, take the Castella exit. Inside the state park (day-use fee), pass through the campground and a mile up steep and narrow but paved Vista Point Road to the trailhead at the top.

McCloud River Falls (3,500')   2   E   *McCloud River, three waterfalls, easy access, good for kids*

For the traveler on I-5, there are few options to get out and really stretch your legs—at least options that don't involve a strenuous trek up a mountainside. Lithia Park in Ashland, maybe, but parking can be a little hectic, especially in the summer Shakespeare season. One of the most delightful secrets in California is about fifteen miles east on State Highway 89, at an easily reached spot where the path is level, and breathtaking waterfalls offer a pleasant respite. Some of California's rivers are workhorses, some have carved dramatic landscapes, but most are just plain pretty, and the prettiest just might be the McCloud, particularly the stretch with Lower, Middle, and Upper Falls.

Famous as a world-class destination for rainbow trout, the McCloud has managed to stay off the radar of most Californians due to being a healthy distance from all major urban areas. The casual walker is fortunate to be offered an easy, well-graded path connecting the three falls in less than two miles. From the Lower-Falls parking area, strike out on any path. The paths to the river all meet a riverside trail on which you turn left (upriver). The profusion of ferns in the gorge here gives it a primeval ambience. Very shortly, the roar of the waterfall is audible, and then Lower Falls appears, spilling fifteen feet over a lip into a large punchbowl formation.

On a warm afternoon, this little piece of paradise will be populated by happy souls of all ages. From the viewpoint, a paved path follows the river upstream, past the campground. Past the campground, the trail becomes well-graded dirt, and a sign indicates that it's 0.5 miles to Middle Falls. The path meanders pleasantly beside the river, which is sometimes obscured by dense riparian undergrowth. As Middle Falls grows nearer, you can glimpse its white curtain through the trees. Near the base of the falls, the trail turns and begins to ascend in switchbacks. Middle Falls, with its fifty-foot Niagara-like drop, is the most spectacular of the three waterfalls here.

For a closer view, you will have to scramble over large, often-slick boulders. Late afternoon is best for photography here. Continuing up the switchbacks and a wooden staircase of thirty-three steps, you'll find yourself one hundred feet above Middle Falls and the river. From here, take either a cliff-top trail or a parallel inland path the short distance to Upper Falls. Impressive in its own way, the thirty-foot waterfall pours through a notch in a wall of basalt. From the fenced viewpoint, it is easy to follow the river rim upstream and peer into the small but rugged gorge. To return to the Lower-Falls parking area, retrace your steps, or arrange for someone to drive around and pick you up at the Upper-Falls viewpoint.

Directions: From I-5, take Highway 89 just south of Mt. Shasta City, 9.0 miles to the small town of McCloud, and then 5.6 miles of arrow-straight highway beyond that to the sign for Fowler Campground / Lower Falls. Turn right (south). At every junction, bear right, finally ending at the parking area for Lower Falls.

Black Butte (6,325') 5.2 M *Panoramic views, Especially Mount Shasta*

Extraordinary views are the reason for tackling this mostly exposed small volcanic cone. Black Butte is that small peak nestled next to Interstate 5 at the base of Mount Shasta. Part of the trail is visible from the interstate. However, as highway rumble is an ongoing reality on much of the trail, the lack of a sense of wilderness is amply compensated.

The trail is a steady ascent through ponderosa pine, incense cedar, Douglas and white firs, winding around the north flank of Black Butte. As you climb, the forest thins on the volcanic soil. Panoramic vistas emerge, looking north across the mountain town of Weed and the Shasta Valley to the Siskiyou range, marking the state line with Oregon. The snow-covered volcanic cone visible beyond the northern sharp-crested mountains is Mount McLoughlin (9,495'). As the trail winds around to the west, Mount Eddy looms to the northeast, and Castle Crags spike the horizon to the south. Just short of 1.5 miles, the trail turns abruptly eastward. It continues its ascent to the summit, winding up around the eastern slopes. After a short series of switchbacks, Black Butte's summit is reached, 2.6 miles from the trailhead. The reward here is the amazing spectacle of Mount Shasta, towering like no other peak in view, the monarch of this neck of the woods.

In spite of the elevation, the trail is mostly exposed and arid. Be sure to have plenty of water and protection from the sun.

Directions: From I-5, take the Central Mount Shasta exit. Head east on Lake Street, continuing as it curves into Everitt Memorial Highway. At 2.9 miles from the interstate, look for the sign for Black Butte Trail on the left. Turn onto a gravel road and follow directional signs for 3.3 miles to the trailhead.

Castle/Heart Lakes (6,050')   3   M   *Lakes, view of Mt. Shasta*

Castle Lake is famous for the purity of its blue water. The very scenic lake is tucked into a natural bowl at 5,200 feet. The trail heads out on the left side of the lake. The views are constant as you climb along a glacial moraine. In a saddle, the trail splits. The left fork heads to Little Castle Lake, and the right fork will take you to Heart Lake. The very picturesque area is lightly forested with firs.

Directions: From I-5 at Mt. Shasta City, follow the signs to Lake Siskiyou, and then the signs to Castle Lake. It is eight miles from Lake Siskiyou to the trailhead at Castle Lake. Mostly forested on both sides, there is a pullout one mile below Castle Lake, which offers an awesome view of Mt. Shasta.

Coast Range—*The Coast Range is almost an afterthought when thinking about hikes. The west side of the Sacramento Valley is not just ignored by tourists. To valley residents, it is merely the western horizon. Few paved highways cross from the valley to the coast. Three peaks loom high enough to be categorized as biological islands, but their trailheads take hours to reach over winding forest roads. Farther south, the trails are easily accessed, but no less uncrowded. The opportunity for true solitude on nearly all Coast Range trails is far greater than any single Sierra trail.*

Berryessa Snow Mountain National Monument
Cold Canyon Loop
Fiske Peak
Frog Pond
Lynch Canyon
Cache Creek Ridge
Redbud Trail
Snow Mountain
Deafy Glade

Black Butte Lake Recreation Area
Orland Buttes
Big Oak Trail

Yolla Bolly Middle Eel Wilderness
South Yolla Bolly
North Yolla Bolly

Stony Creek, Snow Mountain

Berryessa Snow Mountain National Monument
Cold Canyon Loop (1,920') 5.1 M *Coast range canyon, ridge walk, view of Lake Berryessa*

The Cold Canyon Trail is not visible from miles away, but its location is. Looking at the Coast Range from the south valley, the Berryessa Notch, cut by Putah Creek, is clearly defined. From the trailhead, take the main trail to the right into Cold Canyon. (The uphill trail to the left goes up onto the ridge for nice views of the Putah Narrows.) On the main trail, you soon reach the boundary of Stebbins Preserve, under the jurisdiction of UC Davis. The trail follows the east bank of the creek, with many opportunities to access the seasonal stream (quite dry in summer and fall). This portion of the trail is very shady, especially in the morning.

Due to its proximity, Cold Canyon gets a touch of Bay-Area coolness, and the vegetation reflects that. The pungent aroma of bay leaves pervades the air. Midway up the canyon, the trail crosses the creek bed and ascends the still-shaded western bank. Enjoy the shade of the bay laurel grove that fills the canyon because you're about to climb out of it. The trail rises on embedded wood steps to the top of the ridge, to a junction with the Blue Ridge Trail. Turn right and head north along the chaparral-covered crest. Much of the trail is packed earth, but there are uneven rocky sections that make progress slow. The views are expansive across Lake Berryessa.

The incongruous sound of country or rock music can drift up from boats on the lake. In the summer, wisps of coastal overcast are evident over Napa County to the west. At the north end of the ridge, as you begin the descent to the trailhead, a spur trail extends to Eagle Rock for more views of the Putah Narrows and Berryessa Peak on the ridge extending north. The descent is mostly unshaded, which is why the clockwise direction is preferable. Because this is the closest mountain trail to UC Davis, it gets a lot of use.

Directions: From Interstate 505, head about ten miles west from Winters on Highway 128. After crossing Putah Creek below Monticello Dam, look for a large pullout on the right, just before the road curves up toward the dam. There is room for five or six vehicles at the trailhead proper across the highway, but the larger pullout is safer. Use caution when crossing the road on foot.

Fiske Peak (2,868')   8   S   *Views of Sacramento Valley and Cache Creek Narrows, wildflowers*

For a hike with the best reward, this is hard to beat, the place to be on a crystal-clear day. It is the most strenuous trail in the region, so one should be in reasonably good shape to tackle it. Fiske Peak anchors the north end of Blue Ridge, Yolo County's western horizon, extending from Cache Creek to the Putah Creek Narrows. It faces north to Cortina Ridge across the narrows that Cache Creek has carved in its passage out of the mountains into Capay Valley. Walk down to Cache Creek on the old county road and across the low concrete bridge. Cache Creek is a designated wild and scenic river, and this is a rafting take-out point. Cross the bridge and begin looking for the rusted BLM sign for Blue Ridge Trail on the left. This takes you to a narrow, lesser-used, old road, so unused lupine bloom in the middle of the track.

Rounding a bend brings you to the "official" trailhead for the north end of the Blue Ridge Trail. The trail climbs immediately into the oak woodland. For most of the first mile, poison oak crowds the trail. The trail is relentlessly steep with a nearly constant uphill grade for the three miles to the top of the ridge, but the trade-off is the expanding view of Cache Creek Narrows below. In spring, farther up, the trail is lined with wildflowers: shooting stars, Indian warrior, redbud, and especially some of the most abundant displays of Indian paintbrush seen anywhere. At the two-thousand-foot level, two miles up the trail, you can look across the Sacramento Valley to the Sierra Nevada. From this point, the ridge is covered with chaparral and vibrant red paintbrush.

Rounding a bend, you encounter a jumble of boulders, tilted sandstone slabs that look like miniature Easter-Island heads on the loose. It means that you're approaching the top of the ridge and the three-mile point. It is then another mile along the rocky crest to the peak. From Fiske Peak's 2,868-feet summit, the view is sweeping. The eastern ridges of the Coast Range are like the folds of an unmade bed, ancient seabeds pushed and folded into sharp ridges. Glascock Mountain to the north is the clearest example of sandstone strata bent into shape. The vista also encompasses Snow Mountain to the north, Mt. Shasta barely visible as a white bump, Lassen Peak, castle-like Sierra Buttes beyond the Sutter Buttes, and the south Sacramento Valley down to the delta. During spring, the peak is jaw-droppingly festooned with Indian paintbrush.

Directions: On Highway 16, south of Highway 20 and west of I-505, look for the Yolo County Regional Park just above the Cache Creek Narrows, about two miles south of the Colusa County line and the first park site coming from the Capay Valley. Park in the county pay lot or along old Road 40, which is closed to vehicles a short distance from the highway. Road 40 is also known as Rayhouse Road.

Frog Pond   5   M   *Cache Creek, oak woodland, frog pond*

Walk down to Cache Creek on the old county road and across the low concrete bridge. Cache Creek is a designated wild and scenic river, and this is a rafting take-out point. Continue on the old road, past the Blue Ridge Trail turnoff on your left. Three thousand feet above, the north end of Blue Ridge looms. After crossing Fiske Creek, you will pass the red Blue Ridge Barn, built 1890–1910. The road winds through a grove of large oaks to the signed trailhead for Frog Pond. The trail begins climbing immediately. Being an old ranch road, it is wide but designed for horses and wagons, so the climb is steady on what has evolved into a single track.

As the view increases, Cache Creek comes into sight. The trail levels out and becomes a pleasant stroll. There is a fine view of the old red barn and a wide swath of creek canyon. At a junction with the loop, both directions climb, the one to the right less so. Continuing that way, the middle recreation area emerges below, and the climb eases into an even grade. After passing through a pungent grove of bay laurels, the tree curves left and rises out of the shaded tree-covered slope into an open chaparral area extending up the ridge before you. A side trail is marked for Frog Pond. The tiny body of water lives up to its name.

Shadeless, the pond is full of the little bright-green amphibians, either floating or ringing the muddy shore, dozens of little eyes watching you. A small cottonwood on the south side offers the most shade and is a good spot to savor the view of Glascock Mountain anchoring the south end of Cortina Ridge, and farther south, Blue Ridge rising to Fiske Peak. From the pond, the loop continues up through dense chaparral and then reenters the oak and pine woodland, interspersed with open grassland, bringing you to the end of the loop.

Directions: On Highway 16, south of Highway 20 and west of I-505, look for the Yolo County Regional Park just above the Cache Creek Narrows, about two miles south of the Colusa County line and the first park site coming from the Capay Valley. Park in the county pay lot or along old Road 40, which is closed to vehicles a short distance from the highway. Road 40 is also known as Rayhouse Road.

Lynch Canyon   3.4   M   *Oak woodland, small valley, hunter cabin*

This is an easy route into the heart of the Cache Creek Natural Area, oddly not included within the boundaries of the national monument. The trail is a broad ranch road rising uphill through a meadow and across a wide saddle. Beyond, the road drops into wooded Lynch Canyon, winding down into an open valley carpeted with wildflowers in spring.

At 1.7 miles, under a large oak on the southern edge of this valley, is the "Roadkill Cafe," a screen-house hunter's cabin with table and benches. Here you have an option of five different routes. The Ridge Spur and Dunfield Spring trails climb in less than two miles each west to Cache Creek Ridge. Brophy Canyon Trail leads south to Cache Creek Ridge, connecting with High Bridge Trail to Highway 16. Thompson Canyon Trail heads east for Bear Creek and the Cowboy Camp trailhead on Highway 16. The fifth choice is to return up Lynch Canyon to Highway 20.

Directions: Take Highway 20 west from I-5 at Williams. The trailhead is on the left 2.3 miles west of the junction with Highway 16, at the first fishhook bend beyond the Bear Valley vista point.

Cache Creek Ridge (2,200')   2.5–10   M   *Oak woodland, views of Cache Creek area*

A good introduction to this area is a loop up Judge Davis Trail, returning on Cache Creek Ridge Trail. Early morning is best: the light is softer and illuminates the oaks, the air is filled with bird song, and it is cooler in the hot season. Start from the Judge Davis trailhead at the west end of the parking area. Paralleling the highway initially, it then veers away from the busy road and begins its ascent into a pretty canyon, wooded with blue oak and foothill pine.

At a fork, Judge Davis Trail is on the right, heading up the slope. Continue on the left fork for a gentle ascent up the canyon. The cutoff trail climbs gradually to a saddle and junction with Cache Creek Trail. For a quick loop, turn left and drop on the old ranch road to the parking area. For a more leisurely stroll, head to the right and go as far as you wish along the ridge (all the way to Highway 16 if you have a shuttle waiting). The views of the area are commanding. Grassy ridges, chaparral coating the south-facing slopes, stretch in waves to Cortina and Blue Ridge, sharply etched across the eastern horizon. Cache Creek itself is not visible for the first few miles.

Directions: Take Highway 20 west from I-5 at Williams. The trailhead is on the left 4.1 miles west of the junction with Highway 16, shortly after crossing into Lake County.

Redbud Trail 3–6 M *Oak woodland, ridge walk, Cache Creek, spring wildflowers*

The trail begins next to an informational gazebo and winds through a meadow. (A creek-side trail ends at a private property marker about 0.5 miles downstream.) The trail curves to the south side of the meadow, where valley oaks at the base of Perkins Ridge border the meadow. To the north, beyond the creek, erosion has sculpted the hills into a scenic, badlands formation. The trail crosses the broad, normally dry creek bed of Perkins Creek and begins a gradual ascent along slopes wooded with oaks, gray pine, and manzanita. In spring, wildflowers are abundant, including the trail's namesake redbud, brilliant with lavender blossoms.

The trail winds along the slope and bends to follow the spine of a spur ridge to the crest of Perkins Ridge to a trail junction. The left fork is the continuation of Redbud Trail for a mile descending to Baton Flat and the main fork of Cache Creek. A short climb to the right on Perkins Ridge Trail affords a panoramic view of Cache Creek far below and chaparral-covered ridges of the Coast Range rising in all directions. A short distance down the Redbud Trail to Baton Flat, a spur trail signed for Inspiration Point, leads about fifty feet to a dramatic view of the creek twisting through the mountains.

The main trail continues down the crest of the ridge, with constant views into the gorge on the right and the rush of water clearly audible. At the end of Perkins Ridge, the trail drops in broad switchbacks for a gentle descent to the creek. Baton Flat is a large meadow beside Cache Creek, at the base of a ridge, eroded into striated gray badlands. There are a few excellent and well-shaded campsites near the creek. The Redbud Trail continues across Cache Creek to Wilson Valley, where resident tule elk are known to habituate, but with no footbridge, a wade is required to proceed farther. Enjoy the peaceful scenery and return the way you came.

Directions: Take Highway 20 west from I-5 at Williams. The signed turnoff for the trailhead is on the left approximately fifteen miles west of the junction with Highway 16, just after crossing North Fork Cache Creek, and 0.25 miles to reach the trail.

Snow Mountain (7,056') 7.5 M *Botanical island, alpine forest, views*

Snow Mountain is visible to Sacramento Valley residents as the large humplike mass in the Coast Range west of the Sutter Buttes. It is the first sub-alpine peak north of the Bay Area, one of only two in the range. (The other is Mt. Linn in the Yolla Bollys.) Located in Mendocino National Forest, Snow Mountain was designated a federal wilderness in 1984, and in 2015 was included in—and occupies the northernmost portion of—the one-hundred-mile long national monument. The most convenient trailhead for a day hike is Summit Springs closest to the summit and requires the least amount of driving from the valley. The trail begins next to the restroom and drops into a shaded glen of oaks and sugar pines, where you'll find a sign-in sheet (for usage data).

Beyond the trailhead sign, the trail narrows and soon Snow Mountain looms before you. The trail follows the shadeless spur ridge. The views expand: Coast Range ridges to the west, Goat Mountain south. The meeting of the spur ridge and the mountain is also the junction of the Deafy Glade Trail, where it descends to the campground. The Sacramento Valley is now visible. You leave valley views temporarily and traverse the slope, always climbing steadily. Rounding a point, the trail plunges into the shade of a fir-forested canyon and switchbacks up to a narrow ridge crest and the weathered snag of a Jeffery pine etched against the horizon. The trail now ascends gradually along the crest through pine and red fir. Near the main bulk of the mountain, there's a campsite and nice log for a stop to observe the broad valley.

Where the ridge meets the mountain, the forest grows dense. Pass the junction with the trail to Box Springs, into a shaded red fir forest, and soon reach Cedar Camp, a fine campsite at the edge of a meadow. (In spite of the name, there are no cedars here.) The lower meadow is full of corn lilies, and a vernal pond is present after snow melt. At the southwest corner of the campsite is the Milk Ranch Trail. Continue across the upper meadow to, nailed to a tree, a wooden sign for Trail 8W50. The trail wanders up a shaded draw and then to a saddle at 6,600 feet, with the final mile to the summit ahead. From the saddle, cross through the charred remnants of the 2001 Trough Fire. East Peak, your destination, is always visible ahead.

Before the final ascent, the trail crosses a broad meadow, full of corn lilies and bright-yellow mule's ears, and then a glaciated basin, climbing to the summit saddle. At a four-way unsigned junction, turn right for the easy ascent, a stroll at this point, to East Peak. The summit is flat and broad; the view is extraordinary. The valley spreads out, with the Sutter Buttes prominent in the checkerboard of rice fields and orchards. Beyond stretches the North Sierra, Lassen Peak, and Mt. Shasta. To the north, Mt. Linn crowns the horizon. Nearer at hand is St. Johns Mountain, across the portion of Stony Creek Canyon known as Bear Wallow. Far to the west, through a Coast Range gap, Lake Pillsbury can be glimpsed. After taking all this in, retrace your steps to Summit Springs. (This hike can be done from the Deafy Glade trailhead, which adds 3.2 miles of generally steep uphill climbing just to reach the junction with the Summit Springs Trail.)

Directions: Take Maxwell Road west from I-5 at Maxwell, on a winding, paved road over low ridges through the communities of Sites and Lodoga to Stonyford. At Stonyford, turn left onto Fouts Springs Road (Forest Road M-10), signed for Summit Springs. It winds into low hills arid in the mountain's rain shadow. Beyond the former juvenile detention camp, the road winds up through Fouts Springs' off-road vehicle area and into forested elevations. After Dixie Glade campground and the Deafy Glade trailhead, the pavement ends. Road M-10 is wide, well-graded, and very winding, as it follows the mountainside contours. It is 11 miles from pavement end to the junction with Summit Springs Road and then 1.8 miles on that narrow road to the trailhead at 5,250 feet.

Deafy Glade (3,400') 2-6 M *Mixed fir-oak woodland, Stony Creek, Deafy Glade*

This is initially a pleasantly easy and shaded trail for the first mile through a pretty, mixed-oak-fir forest down to South Fork Stony Creek. Just downstream is the confluence with Ladybug Creek, where impressive Deafy Rock rises one hundred feet. There is no footbridge, and in spring and early summer, it may be a challenge to cross; but in autumn, it is easy to hop on rocks. From the creek, the trail climbs for two miles to connect with the Summit Springs Trail to the summit of Snow Mountain.

If that isn't your intention, the creek is a fine place to enjoy the pretty canyon bottom and then return to the trailhead. Or continue up the trail beyond the creek for a quarter mile to Deafy Glade, an open meadow on the steep south slopes. Just as the glade comes into view, look to the right for a faint use-path to a craggy rock outcrop, which provides views of Deafy Rock, Snow Mountain, and the surrounding slopes. There is an alternate trailhead at Dixie Glade Campground, a half mile before the Deafy Glade trailhead.

Directions: Take Maxwell Road west from I-5 at Maxwell, on a winding paved road over low ridges through the communities of Sites and Lodoga to Stonyford. At Stonyford, turn left onto Fouts Springs Road (Forest Road M-10), signed for Summit Springs. It winds into low hills, arid in the mountain's rain shadow. Beyond the former juvenile-detention camp, the road winds up through Fouts Springs' off-road vehicle area and into forested elevations. The Deafy Glade Trailhead, at the end of paved road, is thirteen miles from Stonyford and a half mile beyond Dixie Glade Campground.

Black Butte Lake Recreation Area
Orland Buttes (350') 0.5–6 M *Basalt ridge, views of Sacramento Valley and Black Butte Lake*

Take the trail at the east end of the parking area, up the grassy slope through the visible opening in the fence. It's straight up but isn't long to the top of the black basalt ridge. Across Black Butte Lake is the formation that gave the lake its name. The low ridge is evidence of past volcanic activity. You can follow the ridge on a faint single track for three miles. All the while, the lake, fed by Stony Creek from the slopes of Snow Mountain, stretches out below you. To the east, the north Sacramento Valley extends toward Chico and southeast to the Sutter Buttes. Westward, in the Coast Range, Snow Mountain is visible to the south, as are the Yolla Bollys to the north.

Directions: Take Newville Road / County Road 200 west from I-5 at Orland (Black Butte Lake exit), ten miles to the recreation area. Park in the Eagle Pass parking area.

Big Oak Trail (300')   1   E   *Valley oaks, grassy savannahs*

An easy loop trail wanders through the Stony Creek riparian area at the head of Black Butte Lake. This provides a peaceful stroll among valley oaks, ashes, willows, and an odd grove of bamboo. Wildlife viewing is best at twilight.

Directions: Take Newville Road / County Road 200 west from I-5 at Orland (Black Butte Lake exit), six miles to County Road 206. Turn left and take Road 206, three miles to Road 200A. Turn left onto Road 200A for 3.7 miles to parking on the right.

Yolla Bolly Middle Eel Wilderness—Yolla Bolly is Wintun for "snow-covered peak." Located southwest of Red Bluff, the area encompasses the headwaters of the Middle Eel River. The most daunting aspect here is not the wilderness aspect; it's the drive needed to reach even the most convenient trailheads. You're likely to have any trail to yourself for days if you wish.

South Yolla Bolly (8,094')   3.5–10   M/SC   *Botanical island, alpine forest, Mt. Linn, views*

There's a choice of two trails. It depends on whether your objectives include the summit of Mt. Linn. (If not tackling Mt. Linn, head off on the Ides Cove Trail to Square Lake.) With no formal trails to the peak, access involves cross-country scrambling up the side of the

141

ridge to the crest. The easier approach is from South Yolla Bolly Trail, an old road that follows a level course around the mountain's south flank. Follow it from the trailhead about a half mile to a rocky draw that clefts the ridge up to the crest. It is easier and quicker to zigzag up on animal paths to the left of the draw. At the top, the crest is open and easy to traverse, and the peak is always in sight.

At 8,084 feet, Mt. Linn is the highest point in the Coast Range. The view is spectacular and justifies the effort. Far north are the Trinity Alps, with the ridgeline of the North Yolla Bollys nearer. Pivoting eastward, the vista includes Shasta Bally, Mt. Shasta, Lassen Peak, and the Sierra crest. To the south is the humpbacked mass of Snow Mountain, with conical St. Johns Mountain adjacent. Here on the summit you can find rare foxtail pine, a tree-line species kin to bristlecone pines and endemic only to California.

The two known populations of foxtail are here and in the South Sierra. To now access the Ides Cove Trail below to the north, back-track to the forested side ridge, which extends to tiny Square Lake visible beneath you. It is another cross-country scramble down through a dense forest of fir and Jeffery pine. Pick up the trail just north of the lake and ascend to a burned area and the junction with the Burnt Camp Trail, which drops down the mountainside and offers the option of a shorter loop. The Ides Cove Trail continues, drops a bit, and then climbs to the small basin, where Long Lake sits above, not visible from the trail.

To find the lake, look for its outlet stream and follow that uphill. Continuing onward, the trail passes through a fir forest and, about a mile from Long Lake, reaches a junction with South Yolla Bolly Trail and another option for a loop. It's also the point where the ridge drops, and the Ides Cove Trail dives to the west in its ten-mile loop. This is a good spot to rest and enjoy the view of the Coast Range ridges. If not soldiering on for the entire loop, return to the trailhead via Ides Cove, South Yolla Bolly, or Burnt Camp trails. Due to fire and storm debris, and a general lack of maintenance, there is a primitive aura not apparent at other wildernesses and is a good place to carry a topo map.

Directions: From I-5 at Corning, take Road A-9 west to Paskenta. In Paskenta, turn right on Toomes Creek Road, signed for Ides Cove. After heading straight for a few miles, it then winds up and up where it meets the steep-sloped range and becomes Forest Road M-2. The pavement ends seventeen miles from Paskenta. Follow the signs for Cold Springs Station and Yolla Bolly Wilderness. Six miles farther, at Cold Springs Station, take the right fork, Road M-22, signed for Ides Cove. Roads M-2 and M-22 are both wide and well-graded; parts of M-22 are cliff-huggers. Fifteen miles from pavement's end, watch for Road 25N19 heading uphill to the left.

Curiously, after all the well-placed signs, there is nothing here directing you to the trailhead. A small sign indicates that this spur road is not suitable for low-clearance vehicles, but a passenger car can manage these final two miles. At the trailhead are a couple of pleasantly shaded campsites with tables, but no water or restroom facilities.

North Yolla Bolly (7,863') 8 M *Botanical island, alpine forest, views*

The trail climbs immediately. At a trail junction, ignore the choices for North Yolla Bolly Lake and Barker Camp and continue straight ahead and upward. The trail is alpine-style, meaning up without switchbacks, through a shady fir forest at about six-thousand-foot elevation. Where the trail levels out briefly, the Sacramento Valley can be glimpsed to the east through the dense trees. The trail resumes its uphill ascent with a less severe grade.

After a couple of small meadows, you pass a battered wooden sign indicating the wilderness boundary. Where the trail rounds the shoulder of the mountain, look for a junction with a faint trail on the right, barely noticeable under light debris. The only sign is a small one on a tree pointing to Rat Trap Gap. If your trail begins to descend, you've gone too far. The debris-laden path is the route to the summit. You now proceed on this trail (slowly, if you're kicking debris aside) up the mountain crest, rising gradually. The trail emerges from the forest onto open slopes, with expansive views southward.

At times the trail is barely discernible, but keep heading west, and traces of the trail emerge. The view becomes vaster, looking south to Mt. Linn across the sharp ridges of the wilderness. After a dense stand of red fir, you emerge onto the open ridge with the summit visible ahead. The trail disappears completely, but it's easy to make your way cross-country. An occasional rock cairn is placed as a guide, but they are unnecessary as the ridge is wide open, and the route to the summit is easy to discern. The view from the rocky south summit is remarkable.

To the north across a gap is the slightly higher north summit, which forms a striking frame for the Trinity Alps beyond. Across the Sacramento Valley, Mt. Lassen dominates its portion of the eastern horizon. The peak to the west is Black Rock Mountain, with its old fire lookout on top. The south summit is also home to a small stand of rare foxtail pine. Below just to the east is the Beegum Basin, head-waters of

Beegum Creek. In midsummer, the upper slopes above the basin are carpeted with blue lupine that creates a colorful eyeful to accompany the panorama. Other wildflowers present include crimson Indian paintbrush, magenta bugles, and yellow stars. You can continue rambling around on the summit and return to the trailhead the way you came.

Directions: Take Highway 36 west from I-5 at Red Bluff toward the Coast Range. Turn left on Tedoc Road (Road 45) about 36 from Red Bluff. Stay on Road 45 for eighteen miles to Rat Trap Gap trailhead. The road is unpaved, narrow, and rutty in places, but is manageable by passenger car.

BEST FOR

Wildflowers
Poppy Hill, Spenceville
North Table Mountain
North Rim, Bidwell Park
Buttermilk Bend, Bridgeport
Glacier Lake (Sand Ridge)
Haskell Peak
Mill Creek Falls (trail)
Fiske Peak
Red Bud Trail (Cache Creek)

Wildlife
Feather River Parkway
Bobelaine Sanctuary
Gray Lodge
Colusa
Sacramento NWR
Cosumnes River Preserve
Wood Duck Loop, Spenceville
Jones Pond, Spenceville
Pittman Loop, Spenceville
Four Ponds Loop, Spenceville
Clear Creek Gorge (salmon)

Waterfalls
Hidden Falls
Fairy Falls
Feather Falls
North Table Mountain
Lil Falls, Magalia Greenbelt
Stevens Trail
Rush Creek Falls,
Independence Trail

Historical
Ellis Lake

Fairy Falls (grinding holes)
Pittman Loop (grinding holes)
Clotilde Merlo Park
Lower Bidwell Park ("Robin Hood")
Stevens Trail (railroad)

Bear River Falls, Sierra Discovery Trail

Loves Falls

Frazier Falls

Fern Falls

Brandy Creek Falls

Boulder Creek Falls

Lower Crystal Creek Falls

Whiskeytown Falls

Lower Deer Creek Falls

Mill Creek Falls

Kings Creek Falls

Burney Falls

McCloud River Falls

Hard Rock Trail, Empire Mine

Deer Creek Tribute Trail

Hirschman Pond

Covered Bridges

Rock Creek Nature Trail (mill site)

Diggins Trail (North Bloomfield)

Canyon Creek Trail

Mountain Mine Trail

Lower Salmon Lake (old mine)

Round Lake Loop (old mine)

Cinder Cone / Prospect Peak (Emigrant Trail)

Geology	*Very Easy*	
Fairy Falls	Ellis Lake	Turtle Bay
Lookout Loop, Spenceville	Feather River Parkway	Sacramento River Trail
Council Rocks, Spenceville	Bobelaine Sanctuary	Clear Creek Trail
Rock City, Spenceville	Gray Lodge	Lower Crystal Creek Falls
Bald Rock	Colusa	McCloud River Falls
Bald Dome	Sacramento NWR	Clover Creek Preserve
North Table Mountain	Cosumnes River Preserve	
Upper Bidwell Park		
Diggins Trail, Malakoff Diggins	Ditch Trail, Spenceville	

Loch Leven Lakes

Zion Hill

Island/Penner Lakes

Glacier Lake

Sand Pond Loop

Iron Canyon Loop

Brokeoff Mountain

Bumpass Hell

Lassen Peak

Chaos Crags

Devil's Kitchen

Boiling Lake /
Terminal Geyser

Cinder Cone

Subway Cave

Castle Crags

Black Butte

Mt. Judah

Monkeyface Rock,
Upper Bidwell Park

Waldo Bridge,
Spenceville

Clotilde Merlo Park

Lower Bidwell Park

Hard Rock Trail,
Empire Mine

Hirschman Pond

Covered Bridges

Buttermilk Bend

Independence Trail

Rock Creek
Nature Trail

Sierra Discovery Trail

Loney Meadow

Canyon Creek Trail

Loves Falls

Sand Pond Loop

Frazier Falls

Payne Creek
Wetlands, Big Bend

Handicapped-Access

Ellis Lake

Feather River Parkway

Gray Lodge

Good Intro Hikes

Valley: Gray Lodge

Feather River
Parkway

Bobelaine Audubon
Sanctuary

Sacramento NWR · Cosumnes River Preserve

Cosumnes River Preserve · *Foothills*:
Hidden Falls
Fairy Falls

Clotilde Merlo Park · Council Rocks

Lower Bidwell Park · Rock City

Hirschman Pond · Donovan Hill

Independence Trail · Hard Rock Trail, Empire Mine

Sierra Discovery Trail · Point Defiance Loop

Frazier Falls · Independence Trail

Turtle Bay · North Yuba River Trail

Sacramento River Trail · Loves Falls

Hammon Grove Trail · North Table Mountain
Bald Rock

No Dogs Allowed · *High Country:* Sierra Discovery Trail

Bobelaine Sanctuary · Island Lake

Cosumnes River Preserve · Mt Judah · N Sardine Lake

Clotilde Merlo Park · Frazier Falls

Diggins Trail, Malakoff Diggins · *Red Bluff / Redding*:
Osprey Pond

All trails in Lassen Volcanic NP · Sacramento River Trail

Castle Crags · Clear Creek Greenway
Brandy Creek Falls

Challenging
Road Access

Placer Big Trees Grove

Mosquito Ridge
Rd (20m)

North Yolla Bolly

South Yolla Bolly

Lassen Park Road

above Sulphur Works

Boulder Falls
(steep grade)

Sierra Buttes / PCT
(steep grade)

Southern Cascades:
Lower Deer
Creek Falls

Brokeoff Mountain

Bumpass Hell

Devils Kitchen

Cinder Cone

Hidden Lakes Loop,
Caribou Wilderness

McCloud River Falls

By Elevation (In feet)

Lassen Peak	10,457 feet
Brokeoff Mountain	9,235 (Lassen National Park)
Frog Cliff	8,653 (Donner Pass)
Sierra Buttes	8,591
Bumpass Hell	8,450 (Lassen National Park)
Haskell Peak	8,107 (Sierra Buttes)
South Yolla Bolly	8,092
Cliff/Shadow Lakes	8,050 (Lassen National Park)
Mt. Judah	8,049 (Donner Pass)
North Yolla Bolly	7,863
Mt. Elwell	7,818 (Sierra Buttes)
Grouse Ridge	7,550 (Bowman Lake Road)
Deer Lake	7,090 (Sierra Buttes)
Snow Mountain	7,056
Mountain Mine	7,020 (Sierra Buttes)

Round Lake Loop	7,020	(Sierra Buttes)
Spanish Peak	6,975	(Bucks Lake Wilderness)
Cinder Cone	6,907	(Lassen National Park)
Hidden Lakes Loop	6,880	(Caribou Wilderness)
Island Lake	6,875	(Bowman Lake Road)
Loch Leven Lakes	6,870	(Tahoe National Forest)
Terminal Geyser	6,250	(Lassen National Park)
Zion Hill	6,201	(Bowman Lake Road)
Frazier Falls	6,180	(Sierra Buttes)
Fern Falls	6,160	(Sierra Buttes)
Loney Meadow	6,000	(Bowman Lake Road)
Sand Pond	5,762	(Sierra Buttes)
Devils Kitchen	5,760	(Lassen National Park)
Placer Big Trees	5,310	(Tahoe National Forest)
Loves Falls, North Yuba	4,800	(Sierra City)
Sierra Discovery Trail	4,560	(Bowman Lake Road)
Deer Creek Falls	3,600	(Lassen National Forest)
Clotilde Merlo Park	3,570	(Paradise Ridge)
Tehama Wildlife Area	3,500	(Tehama Foothills)
Bald Rock	3,274	
Malakoff Diggins	3,080	
Whiskeytown Falls	3,000	(Whiskeytown Lake)
Fiske Peak	2,850	(Cache Creek)
Hirschman Pond	2,653	(Nevada City)
Empire Mine	2,500	(Grass Valley)
Magalia Greenbelt	2,460	(Paradise Ridge)
Stevens Trail	2,425	(Colfax)
Ryan Preserve	2,410	(Grass Valley)
Castle Crags	2,400	
North Yuba Trail	2,200	(Downieville)
Feather Falls	1,942	

Donovan Hill	1,630 (Yuba Foothills)
North Table Mountain	1,320 (Oroville)
Upper Bidwell	1,263 (Chico)
Hidden Falls	1,100 (Auburn)
Rose Hill	1,056 (Spenceville)
Black Swan Preserve	1,000 (Smartville)
Lookout Loop	820 (Spenceville)
Rock City	651 (Spenceville)
Fairy Falls	600 (Spenceville)
Bridgeport	563 (South Yuba River)
Sacramento River	472 (Redding)
Lower Bidwell	197 (Chico)
Gray Lodge	62
Yuba City	52

ABOUT THE AUTHOR

John Elliott's first memory is as a toddler racing off to explore Elephant Rock in Missouri (until being scooped up by his father). Always ready to see what is around the next bend, he finds every trail to be a rabbit hole leading to another wonderland. With a degree in Religious Studies from Lewis & Clark College, Portland, Oregon, John prepared for the ministry but opted instead to go hiking on Sunday mornings. Life has taken him from the Midwest to the West Coast, from Southern California to Seattle, including Santa Cruz, Las Vegas, and Finegold. Since 2002, he has made his home in the Sacramento Valley town of Yuba City, California.

9 781684 568666